Neoism, Plagiarism & Praxis

by Stewart Home

AK PRESS

EDINBURGH & SAN FRANCISCO • 1995

Neoism, Plagiarism & Praxis by Stewart Home
A CIP catalogue for this book is available from the British Library
A catalogue entry for this book is available from the Library of Congress

Much of the material included in this volume has previously appeared elsewhere.
Published in 1995 by AK Press Edinburgh and San Francisco

AK Press, 22 Lutton Place, Edinburgh, Scotland, EH8 9PE, UK.
AK Press, P. O. Box 40682, San Francisco, CA 94140-0682, USA.

ISBN 1 873176 33 3

Stewart Home can be contacted directly at BM Senior, London WC1N 3XX, UK (full address) or via the publishers.

Printed in the Great Britain.

Contents

Introduction

"True and false belongs to speech, and not to things, And from hence it is evident, that truth and falsity have no place but amongst living creatures as use speech."
Thomas Hobbes

THE TEXTS COLLECTED IN THIS VOLUME are an unrepresentative selection of my writing from the mid-eighties onwards. Much of what I've written about the avant-garde is repetitious and it would be pointless to reprint this material in its entirety. *The Assault on Culture* incorporates some of my earlier work on the subject and I refer interested readers to that book. A number of the pieces included here have been re-edited to avoid too great an overlap between them. Therefore, if this book is still found to be repetitious, it will have served its purpose by proving Kierkegaard's dictum that: 'Boredom is the daemonic side of pantheism... Boredom is partly an inborn talent, partly an acquired immediacy. The English are in general the paradigmatic nation. A true talent for indolence is very rare; it is never met with in nature, but belongs to the world of the spirit. Occasionally, however, you will meet a travelling Englishman who is, as it were, the incarnation of this talent – a heavy, immovable animal, whose entire language exhausts its riches in a single word of one syllable.'

The pieces in the first section of this volume run more or less chronologically from 1986 to 1989 and are taken from *The Art Strike Handbook* and later issues of *Smile*. Two of these works, *Karen Eliot* and *Demolish Serious Culture*, were collective productions. The next section consists of articles that accompanied various exhibitions and installations. This is followed by two 'Neoist' texts. The *Correspondence Script* is another collaborative work, assembled from letters sent to Pete Horobin and myself, it has been revised since it was first published in 1985. Despite its fictional form, *Retro-Futurism* (originally published in 1985) is the most extensive record so far produced of the *Eighth International Neoist Apartment Festival*. A factual account of a more substantial poly-media manifestation of the eighties avant-garde can be found in my *Festival of Plagiarism* pamphlet. Readers interested in Neoism should also check out my *Neoist Manifestos* and forthcoming novel *Slow Death*.

The final section of this book is given over to writing produced since the end of the Art Strike. In these texts, I begin to historicise the avant-garde of the eighties, as well as writing about contemporary manifestations of anti-institutional culture. Appended to this are conversations about my activities conducted by Karen Goaman and Simon Ford. The latter is one of the few people to understand that by openly campaigning for the Neoist, Plagiarist and Art Strike movements to be incorporated into the collections of leading museums, I'm deterring curators from touching this material. Most art administrators don't like the ways in which they operate to be openly talked about, they'd much rather I remained silent on the subject, so that my work could be shrouded in reverence. In a third appendix there is a selection of my correspondence from 1989, hopefully this gives some insight into how the Art Strike was organised. This is followed by the *Introduction to the Polish Edition of The Assault on Culture*, an unveiling of the occult influences upon oppositional culture.

This book does not provide an exhaustive account of the eighties avant-garde, a great deal remains to be written on the subject. For example, I am unaware of anything having been published that traces the use of the collective names Karen Eliot and Monty Cantsin back through the adoption of Emmett Grogan as a multiple identity by a number of the San Francisco Diggers in the 1960s. For the benefit of those not in the know, Praxis was little more than a paper organisation consisting of myself with occasional back up from John Berndt. In contrast to this, the Neoist, Plagiarist and Art Strike movements were just as substantial as the earlier Dadaist, Surrealist and Situationist groups, all of which were numerically insignificant when compared to the following for Spiritualism or top-flight New Age gurus. As Nietzsche observed: 'the point of honesty is deception, with all great deceivers there is a noteworthy occurrence to which they owe their power. In the actual act of deception... they are overcome by belief in themselves... Men believe in the truth of things that are plainly and strongly believed'. As for the avant-garde, it is closer to Stirner's weltanschauung: 'Whether I am in the right or not there is no judge but myself. Others can judge only whether they endorse my right, and whether it exists as right for them too'. Belief is the enemy, it provides the means by which we can articulate our thoughts while simultaneously robbing them of vitality and vigour. I have always been fascinated by deceit and the texts collected here are a direct reflection of this interest.

Stewart Home, London
September 1994

Part

From Plagiarism to Praxis

Karen Eliot

KAREN ELIOT IS A NAME THAT REFERS to an individual human being who can be anyone. The name is fixed, the people using it aren't. Smile is a name that refers to an international magazine with multiple origins. The name is fixed, the types of magazines using it aren't. The purpose of many different magazines and people using the same name is to create a situation for which no one in particular is responsible and to practically examine western philosophical notions of identity, individuality, originality, value and truth.

Anyone can become Karen Eliot simply by adopting the name, but they are only Karen Eliot for the period in which the name is used. Karen Eliot was materialised, rather than born, as an open context in the summer of '85. When one becomes Karen Eliot one's previous existence consists of the acts other people have undertaken using the name. When one becomes Karen Eliot one has no family, no parents, no birth. Karen Eliot was not born, s/he was materialised from social forces, constructed as a means of entering the shifting terrain that circumscribes the 'individual' and society.

The name Karen Eliot can be strategically adopted for a series of actions, interventions, exhibitions, texts, etc. When replying to letters generated by an action/text in which the context has been used then it makes sense to continue using the context, i.e. by replying as Karen Eliot. However in personal relationships, where one has a personal history other than the acts undertaken by a series of people using the name Karen Eliot, it does not make sense to use the context. If one uses the context in personal life there is a danger that the name Karen Eliot will become over-identified with individual beings.

Demolish Serious Culture

WE CALL ON ALL CULTURAL WORKERS to put down their tools and cease to make, distribute, sell, exhibit, or discuss their work from January 1st 1990 to January 1st 1993. We call for all galleries, museums, agencies, 'alternative' spaces, periodicals, theatres, art schools &c., to cease all operations for the same period.

Art is conceptually defined by a self-perpetuating elite and marketed as an international commodity. Those cultural workers who struggle against the reigning society find their work either marginalised or else co-opted by the plutocratic art establishment.

The ruling class uses art as a 'transcendental' activity in the same way it once used religion to justify the arbitrariness of its enormous privilege. Art creates the illusion that, through activities which are actually waste, this civilisation is in touch with 'higher sensibilities' that redeem it from accusations of exploitation and mass murder. Those who accept this logic support the plutocracy even if they are economically excluded from the class. The idea that 'everything is art' is the height of this smoke-screen, meaning only that certain members of the ruling class feel particularly free in expressing their domination of the masses to one another.

To call one person an 'artist' is to deny another the equal gift of vision; thus the myth of 'genius' becomes an ideological justification for inequality, repression and famine. What an artist considers to be his or her identity is a schooled set of attitudes; preconceptions that imprison humanity in history. It is the roles derived from these identities, as much as the art products mined from reification, that we must reject.

Unlike Gustav Metzger's Art Strike of 1977–1980, our intention is not to destroy those institutions that might be perceived as having a negative effect on artistic production. Instead, we intend to question the role of the artist itself and its relation to the dynamics of power within contemporary society.

Desire in Ruins

1 The whole of post-modern life is mediated by a series of abstractions. Creativity, pleasure, imagination, desire, all have a role to play in the maintenance of the capitalist system.

2 Those who do not reiterate accepted mystifications find their activities and ideas suppressed by both the media and the soft cops in the universities and community relations.

3 In the past, life was mediated by such abstractions as honesty, truth, progress, and the myth of a better future. Creativity, pleasure, imagination and desire are a further refinement of this process. In the post-modern era, they serve the same function as progress &c., in the classical modern age (1909-1957).

4 Creativity is labour reified to moral good; the name of the work ethic after its modernisation. To those who oppose all moralisms, creativity is just as alienating as wage labour. We reiterate the anti-moralist slogan 'Never Work' and hold that this formulation embraces the refusal of creativity.

5 Pleasure is a method for the ordering of experience into a hierarchy of desirability. It is an abstraction that negates the lived moment and requires reference to the possibility of past/future (or at least other) experience. We must reject all such systems of value.

6 Imagination is an abstraction that negates concrete experience. It is the central mechanism for the dominance of the image as chief agent of repression in our spectacular society.

7 Desire is the permanent deferral of the actuality of the present in favour of the purported gratifications of an illusory future.

8 We engage an active nihilism for the destruction of this world and all its abstractions:
No more leaders.
No more experts.
No more politicos.
No more thinking 'culture' can change anything except a few bank accounts.
The show is over.
The audience start to leave.
Time to collect their coats and go home.
They turn around...
...No more coats!
...No more homes!

ABOLISH PLEASURE
REFUSE CREATIVITY
SMASH THE IMAGINATION
DESIRE IN RUINS
THE PRESENT IS ABSOLUTE
EVERYTHING NOW!

The art of ideology and the ideology of art

"Business art is the step that comes after art. I started as a commercial artist, and I want to finish as a business artist... Being good in business is the most fascinating kind of art... making money is art and working is art and good business is the best art."
Andy Warhol

The art of criticism

"... the desire for an authentic life serves as one example of where there is a potential of a radical break with the values of this society."
Kevin H. – The Real Thing in *Here and Now*, issue 2

THE DESIRE FOR AUTHENTICITY is the most cynical of all the pseudo-needs manufactured by bourgeois ideologists. Capitalism offers up the spectacle of its own inadequacy and then uses this spectacle as the means of reselling itself to those who 'imagine' they have 'progressed' beyond bourgeois values in a 'return' to the 'authentic'. From health food to anarchism we are bombarded with a thousand and one alternative forms of misery: and while those who believe themselves to be 'different' and 'individual' cling desperately to their 'own' pseudo-brand of 'authenticity', there are others who recognise the social nature of (wo)mankind, the necessity of communist revolution and of a radical break with bourgeois values.

The criticism of art

"In art theory those who would avoid a simple inversion of the code raise themselves to a position of superiority that surveys codes."
John Young and Terry Blake
On Some Alternatives To The Code In The Age Of Hyperreality

WHILE THOSE WHO MAKE A LIVING from the pseudo-criticism of art choose to rise above commitment to life, there are others who take the distinction between the present and its permanent deferral seriously. The latter are committed to the abolition of time and all other social abstractions; in particular the privileged sphere of 'art'. The work of art is never produced but always reproduced from the reifications of bourgeois ideology. Supposedly rising above ideological constructions, the work of art actually descends beneath them to the lowest layer of ideological production; from this point it can more effectively partake in the endless reproduction of capitalist 'social' relations. Spawn of bourgeois mystification, art must necessarily disappear when the social system it supports is overthrown. The successful completion of proletarian revolution will coincide with the abolition of art and all other forms of creativity and 'self-expression'.

Authentic ideology

"Seeing the Sex Pistols for the first time was like awakening from a 14 year sleep. Or so it seemed, but then I never really saw the Pistols, I never saw them live, I only saw tv footage."
Mike Kemp – Punk In The Suburbs

THERE IS NOTHING THAT MAKES seeing a pop group in a club or concert hall more 'real' than watching them on a tv screen. However, under capitalism television is simultaneously promoted as the 'universal' medium of technological society and yet somehow 'inferior' to the very communication systems it has replaced. Thus what should have been rendered obsolete is magically granted a privileged status on the grounds that it is somehow more 'authentic'. But then as anybody who has been on the scene of a disaster knows, these events only gain any real power once they have been processed by the media. The ideology of the 'authentic' is used to sell us the pseudo-alternative of the out-dated; simultaneously it reinforces bourgeois social relations by presenting us with the spectacle of choice under Capital.

The Art of Refusal and the Refusal of Art

"We must liquidate this crazy thing called art to make it possible for all people everywhere to be creative. It is our duty to become self-destructive in a constructive way. We must liquidate not only our own function as artists but we must liquidate the art system as well.'
From the Manifesto of The International Coalition for the Liquidation of Art

TO DEMAND THE DESTRUCTION of art in the name of creativity is merely a reform of Power. To trade off art against creativity is to take back with one hand what has been rejected by the other. Those who genuinely oppose alienated social relations will not only break with art but affirm the refusal of creativity.

The Art of Suffering and Suffering for Art

"The arts are a growing concern. They enrich the quality of our lives. And they enrich us financially too."
From a leaflet issued by The National Campaign for the Arts

WHAT 'INDIVIDUAL' ARTISTS SUFFER in the creation of bourgeois ideology is nothing compared to the damage they inflict on society as a whole. If artists suffer they cannot suffer enough; they deserve all the horrors of hell. It is high time these pathetic excuses for humanity learnt that the world doesn't revolve around them; that it is quite natural that proletarians, who are locked in mortal combat with the bourgeois patrons of 'serious culture', should only take a negative and destructive interest in works of art.

International campaign for the Abolition of Work and All Forms of Creativity

"Through the production of an art commodity, the artist has become a businessman. In order to market his commodity and increase its commercial value, he must create a mystique about himself and his work. The gallery is the means through which the commodity is dispensed. The museum serves the purpose of sanctifying both the commodity and the artist. The collector is the stock speculator. The corporation patrons use the commodity as a sanctification and sanitization of their image. The art magazines are the trade journals, the financial reports of the art world. And the critic serves the function of whip hand for all."

Guerrilla Art Action Group – Toward A New Humanism

Those of us who will be making a total break with all forms of creativity between 1990 and 1993 are not interested in the new humanisms of individuals who speak so as not to be. For a minimum of three years we will not create art, texts or philosophies. Since we are interested in the destruction of this society, we view the humanists of both left and right – imbeciles seeking petty reforms – as our avowed enemies, whose liquidation will be necessary before we can dissolve this world of appearances.

Beneath the cobblestones, the sewers

SINCE THE TIME OF PLATO, when the malign influence of Socrates first entered Western thought, philosophers have sought to reduce (wo)mankind to the banality of coherence. It is not surprising that the concept of the subconscious was later introduced as an occult organising principle.

For us, it is enough to have read Debord to be able to quote Marx citing Hegel. We have studiously avoided reading Hegel in the original and we are under no illusions as to the reactionary nature of 'scientific socialism'. Social science is paternalism materialised.

It has become a commonplace that philosophy is to literature what slapstick is to comedy. Only the most lumpen elements in this society have resisted the implications of this cliché.

Taste, like law, is based on precedent. It is no longer possible to imagine that the future will be any different from the past. Doesn't the preceding sentence strike you as something that anyone might have written?

From Dada to Class War:

ten minutes that shook cheque book journalism

EVER SINCE 'GROWN-UP MEN' started reading Lautreamont, there has existed a confusion between art (a way of looking at the world) and politics (a way of forcing the masses to accept a particular world view). In 1924, Pope Andre Breton, a parish priest of the imagination, dealt Dada a blow from which it never recovered by renaming it Surrealism. Before Breton succeeded in killing the Dadaist dream with a deadly injection of Trotskyite ideology, several of his cohorts departed for the Holy Church of Stalinism.

The links between Surrealism and its bastard offspring, the Situationist International, are too well known for us to go over them again. All that needs to be said is that through a massive dose of subjectivity, the Situationists managed to convinced themselves – and a handful of students – that they'd superseded art and paved the way for a world wide proletarian revolution with unlicensed pleasure as its only aim. In fact, what the Situationists had actually done, was supersede art with literature.

Today, there are many groups, both artistic and political, who have inherited something from this tradition. For example, both the Neoists and Class War would do virtually anything to gain a few paragraphs of scandalised press coverage. The Neoists play the art stage, one of them recently pointed out to an art gallery attendant that he'd thrown a vial of his own blood over a Montreal museum wall. He was hoping to be arrested but the gallery curator and his security team chose to ignore the incident. Class War play the political stage and do much better than the Neoists in terms of media coverage. They are the true heirs of Dada.

From author to authority:

Pepsi versus Coke

IN THE BEGINNING THERE WAS primitive community. Perhaps even then, there were practices established by tradition that institutionalised Power. Of course, a leader has always had to be strong – but this has never been simply a question of physical strength – more important is mental agility and a correct alignment of character armour. As a consequence, there will always be a difference between theory and ideology. While ideologies are constructed by those in Power, or those who overtly seek Power, theorists create situations in which their covert bids for Power are masked by a cloak of pseudo-invisibility. Theorists begin as authors and end up as authorities.

If you want a vision of the future, imagine the present extended indefinitely. In keeping with the dynamic of self-managed 'alienation' so dear to democratic 'capitalism', categories such as 'communication, participation and play' are quite deliberately confused with their polar opposite – life. Accordingly, the theorists of 'liberation' will continue marketing this formula as the negation of 'alienation' - all the while offering us a choice between brand X (situationism) and brand Y (liberalism).

Artist's placement and the end of art

"Artists' Placement is intended to serve Art rather than to provide a service for artists."
Barbara Steveni – Will Art Influence History? In *AND Journal of Art* N° 9

IN THE ARTICLE FROM WHICH this quote is extracted, Steveni elaborates that the 'APG (Artists' Placement Group) was never created as an agency to help artists find employment, or to create new forms of support for artists. APG is a means of generating change through the media of art rather than through verbal proceedings only, in the context of organisation.' Thus the APG seeks to propagate the concept of the placement of artists in government and industry. The 'placed artist' is to play the role of 'incidental person' and carry an open brief.

Such aims are at best reformist. For those who do not adhere to a 'revolutionary perspective' the idea of placing 'incidental persons' in government and industry might appear 'radical' if the concept were removed from the conservative framework within which the APG attempt to contain it.

Close examination of the APG's theory shows that in terms of its actual practice, the propagation of the concept of artists as 'incidental persons' is only a second order activity. The APG's first priority is clearly the maintenance of a belief in 'Art', and the role of the artist, in a society where such mystifications are increasingly viewed as irrelevant, not only by the general population, but also by those whose system 'Art' supports.

In effect, the APG is calling for the utilisation of specialists (artists) in a non-specialist role (the 'incidental person'). Thus the APG hope to create for themselves (artists) a preserve as professional non-specialists, while excluding ordinary workers and the unemployed from fulfilling any 'incidental' function.

The APG are a professional self-interest group. Like all artists, they stand in opposition to the aims and aspirations of the impossible class.

Neoism

NEOISM WAS A CULTURAL MOVEMENT influenced by Futurism, Dada, Fluxus and Punk, which emerged from the Mail Art Network in the late seventies. The initial idea came from the US Mail Artists David Zack and Al Ackerman, but the fledgling movement found its focus in Montreal (Spring 1979). The Montreal group wanted to escape from 'the prison of art' and 'change the world'. With this end in mind, they presented society with an angst-ridden image of itself. Their activities are typified by Kiki Bonbon's film *Flying Cats*. Two men, dressed in white coats, stand on top of a tower block. They have with them a selection of cats. One at a time, the cats are picked up and thrown to their death. Throughout the film, the protagonists repeat the phrase 'the cat has no choice'.

The Neoists tended to use the mediums of video, audio and live performance. They developed the concept of Apartment Festivals as a way of showing such work. These were week long events based in the living spaces of individual Neoists. The first of these was held in Montreal in September 1980. Subsequent Apartment Festivals took place in Baltimore (twice), Toronto, New York (twice), London, Ponte Nossa (Italy), Berlin and Montreal (twice more).

By the summer of 1981, the centre of Neoist activity had shifted to Baltimore (Maryland, USA) and was focused on Michael Tolson (who worked under the names Tim Ore and tENTATIVELY a cONVENIENCE). Tolson is self-described as a 'mad scientist/d composer/sound thinker/ t hought collector/as been & not an artist'. He is best known for his *Pee Dog/Poop Dog Copyright Violation*, which he performed on behalf of the Church of the SubGenius in September 1983. The event made national news when Baltimore police discovered him stark naked beating a dead dog in a railway tunnel, with an audience of 35 people watching.

The Neoist Network held its first European Training Camp in Wurzburg,

Germany, in June 1982. This led to the involvement of the Scottish artist Pete Horobin, who went on to organise the *8th Neoist Apartment Festival* in London (1984) and the *9th Neoist Festival* in Ponte Nossa, Italy (1985). However, after a few years of frantic activity, all the members of the small British group renounced Neoism. The last big Neoist event was the *64th (sic) Apartment Festival* organised by Graf Haufen and Stiletto in Berlin, December 1986. However, with the withdrawal of the British section and apathy on the part of most North Americans, Neoism appears to be a spent force.

Art Strikes

IN HIS SECTION OF the *Art Into Society/Society Into Art* catalogue (ICA, London 1974), Gustav Metzger issued a call for a three-year strike by artists. Metzger believed that if artists acted in solidarity, they could destroy those institutions (such as Cork Street) which had a negative effect on artistic production. Metzger's strike failed because he was unable to mobilise support from other artists.

During martial law in Poland, artists refused to exhibit their work in state galleries, leaving the ruling elite without an official culture. For months the art galleries were empty. Eventually some mediocre artists were discovered who were prepared to take advantage of this situation and their work was shown. The Polish intelligentsia immediately organised an effective boycott of openings, denying the art an audience and the bureaucracy any credibility.

In 1985 the Praxis group proposed an Art Strike for the three years between 1990 and 1993. In 1986 this proposal was extended to a more generalised 'refusal of creativity'. The idea was not to destroy the art world, Praxis doubted that enough solidarity existed between artists for such a strategy to work. Praxis were interested in how they, and many other 'activists' had created identities based on the supposed 'superiority' of their 'creativity' and/or political actions to the leisure and work pursuits of the social majority. This belief in individual superiority was seen as impeding a rigorous critique of the reigning society. Put bluntly, those whose identity is based on 'their opposition' to the world as it is, have a vested interest in maintaining the status quo. To change the world it is necessary to abandon those character traits that aid survival in capitalist society.

Art Strike 1990–1993

WHEN THE PRAXIS GROUP DECLARED their intention to organise an Art Strike for the three year period 1990–1993, they fully intended that this proposed (in)action should create at least as many problems as it resolved.

The importance of the Art Strike lies not in its feasibility but in the possibilities it opens up for intensifying the class war. The Art Strike addresses a series of issues; most important amongst these is the fact that the socially imposed hierarchy of the arts can be actively and aggressively challenged. Simply making this challenge goes a considerable way towards dismantling the mental set 'art' and undermining its hegemonic position within contemporary culture, since the success of art as a supposedly 'superior form of knowledge' is largely dependant upon its status remaining unquestioned.

Other issues with which the Art Strike is concerned include that series of 'problems' centred on the question of 'identity'. By focusing attention on the identity of the artist and the social and administrative practices an individual must pass through before such an identity becomes generally recognised, the organisers of the Art Strike intend to demonstrate that within this society there is a general drift away from the pleasures of play and simulation; a drift which leads, via codification, on into the prison of the 'real'. So, for example, the role-playing games of 'children' come to serve as preparation for the limited roles 'children' are forced to 'live' out upon reaching 'maturity'. Similarly, before an individual can become an artist (or nurse, toilet cleaner, banker &c.), they must first simulate the role; even those who attempt to maintain a variety of possible identities, all too quickly find their playful simulations transformed (via the mechanics of law, medical practice, received belief &c.) into a fixed role within the prison of the 'real' (quite often literally in the case of those who are branded schizophrenic).

The organisers of the Art Strike have quite consciously exploited the fact that within this society what is simulated tends to become real. In the economic sphere, the strike is an everyday action; by simulating this classic tactic of proletarian struggle within the realm of culture we can bring the everyday reality of the class war to the attention of the 'avant-garde' fraction within the bourgeoisie (and thus force academics, intellectuals, artists &c. to demonstrate whose side they are really on). At present the class struggle is more readily apparent in the consumption of culture (cf. Bourdieu) than in its production; the Art Strike is in part an attempt to redress this imbalance.

While strikes themselves have traditionally been viewed as a means of combating economic exploitation, the Art Strike is principally concerned with the issue of political and cultural domination. By extending and redefining traditional conceptions of the strike, the organisers of the Art Strike intend to increase its value both as a weapon of struggle and a means of disseminating proletarian propaganda. Obviously, the educative value of the strike remains of primary importance; its violence helps divide the classes and leads to a direct confrontation between antagonists. The deep feelings aroused by the strike bring out the most noble qualities of the proletariat. Thus both the General Strike and the Art Strike should be understood in terms of social psychology, as intuitive mental pictures rather than actions that have been rationally theorised.

In 1985, when the PRAXIS group declared their intention to organise an Art Strike for the period 1990 - 1993, it resolved the question of what members of this group should do with their time for the five year period leading up to the strike. This period has been characterised by an on-going struggle against the received culture of the reigning society (and has been physically manifested in the adoption of multiple identities such as Karen Eliot and the organisation of events such as the *Festival Of Plagiarism*). What the organisation of the Art Strike left unresolved was how members of PRAXIS and their supporters should use their time over the period of the strike. Thus the strike has been positioned in clear opposition to closure - for every 'problem' it has 'resolved', at least one new 'problem' has been 'created'.

Work

UNDER CAPITAL, THE ATOMISED INDIVIDUAL is coerced into the role of worker and/or house-wife. This process begins at birth. Children are encouraged to take on stereo-typical roles (i.e. doctor, nurse, postman, mother) and 'play' them out. In this way children learn to create self-images based on the approved models of capitalist society; their personalities moulded to prepare them for wage-slavery and/or the unpaid drudgery of house-work. As children grow-up, they're pressured into selecting a job based on their parents socio-economic position.

Work and identity are fused by and for the benefit of capital. The roles of worker and house-wife become mechanisms of social use and potential profit. Personal traits are viewed as simultaneously attributable to, and responsible for, each individuals' socio-economic position. At work each individual is reduced to their potential for productivity - and thus profit.

To deal with the alienation that work creates, the image makers who service the ruling class (i.e. journalists, artists &c.) have long strived to mystify the difference between work (which creates value) and capital (which appropriates value). Workers are encouraged to feel a sense of enjoyment and satisfaction (pride in the job) from the execution of boring, repetitive, and often pointless tasks. This sense of pride (alongside a self-image generated from occupation) is used to both mask and justify the appropriation of value (profit). According to this conceit, human beings need purposeful activity in order to live; and work supposedly fulfils this need.

Oppositional culture and cultural opposition

'ART' AS A CATEGORY HAS 'TRADITIONALLY' been viewed as autonomous of class, economic and political conflicts; recently there's been a growing recognition that the mental set 'art' is directly linked to snobbery and an acritical celebration of bourgeois lifestyles. Of particular interest in this field are two books which were first published in the late seventies; Roger L. Taylor's *Art, An Enemy Of The People* (Harvester Press, Hassocks 1978) and *Distinction: A Social Critique Of The Judgement Of Taste* by Pierre Bourdieu (first published by Les Editions de Minuit, Paris 1979, English translation published by Routledge & Kegan Paul, London 1984). The arguments in these two tomes not only illuminate the 'real' function of art, but also provide us with conceptual tools for understanding what actually constitutes a revolt against art and the bourgeois order in general. I will give an extremely bastardised version of the arguments in these books (taking what I find useful from each text and ignoring a number of divergences between them) which can then be used to assist our understanding of groups such as the Situationists, Fluxus and the Neoists.

Art, as a category, took on its modern meaning in the eighteenth century. The aristocracy were the first class to separate the objects contained within various disciplines and elevate a minority of them to the status of 'art'. At this time beauty was seen as being directly linked to 'truth'. Truth was the world order of the aristocracy – in which everything had a correct and hierarchicised place – and art consisted of the reproduction of this world order in the disciplines of painting, literature, music &c.

Art, in this modern sense, was a reaction on the part of the aristocracy to the development of bourgeois science. It was an attempt on the part of a threatened class to create a system of knowledge that could rival that of science. The bourgeoisie as a rising, and ultimately victorious class, wanted to take over the lifestyles of the aristocracy – but the effects of the bourgeois revolution tended to eliminate the previous modes of existence. Thus when the bourgeoisie came to appropriate the category of art from the defeated aristocratic class, they simultaneously transformed it. Beauty ceased to be a question of 'truth' and came to be understood as a matter of 'individual' taste. To the bourgeoisie, art was a superior form of knowledge; and simultaneously an intellectual system that celebrated the bourgeois lifestyle as being 'objectively' superior to that of any other epoch or class.

However, the bourgeoisie were (and are) not a unified class – as is demonstrated by the on-going struggles between those in positions of economic and political power and those in positions of cultural power. The latter fraction are forever invoking the name of the people in the pursuit of their cause – but as we shall see, their activities are actually opposed to the interests of the proletariat and objectively reinforce the domination of the bourgeois class as a whole over the proletarian majority.

Those who hold positions of economic and political power tend to be more conservative in their cultural tastes than those who hold positions of cultural power (academics, artists and intellectuals). However, the essential distinction is still between bourgeois taste and popular taste. Contemporary bourgeois taste is based on aesthetic distancing. Thus in theatre we find that the bourgeoisie appreciate Brechtian devices which constantly remind the audience that they are watching a play, a piece of make-believe. Bourgeois taste demands formal innovation, emphasis on form and as far as possible, the liquidation of any meaningful content. This reflects the bourgeois desire to master the world rather than identify with it, and finds a perfect expression in abstract painting, post modernism and the writings of Beckett and Robbe-Grillet. In contemporary popular taste, form is subordinated to function; the popular audience demand 'plots that proceed logically and chronologically towards a happy end, and identifies better with simply drawn situations and characters' (see Bourdieu page 32).

If we turn our attention to some manifestations of 'oppositional culture' we now have a conception of art against which we can measure counter-cultural theories and practices. Since pre-war examples (Futurism, Dada, Surrealism) are relatively well known – and to go over their history yet again would prove rather tedious – I will instead examine three post-war 'anti-art' groupings beginning with the Situationist International (SI). This organisation was founded in 1957 from the amalgamation of two small avant-garde groups; the Lettriste International and the International

Movement For An Imaginist Bauhaus. The Lettriste International had been a break-away group from Isidore Isou's Lettriste Movement. Isou's group had been chiefly concerned with producing a form of visual literature that resembles concrete poetry (and which the lettristes believed resystematised all the sciences of language and the sign) and experimental films (the 'innovations' introduced included the use of deliberately boring footage). The Lettriste International had moved away from experimental literature to the production of short theoretical texts – chiefly concerned with the cinema, art, urbanism &c. The International Movement For An Imaginist Bauhaus had also been concerned with the production of theoretical texts, but its members had also been prolific in producing works of fine art (chiefly paintings and ceramics).

By 1962 the SI had split into two factions – the one calling itself the 2nd Situationist International was based on the Situationist Bauhaus (a farm house in southern Sweden), the other was centred on Paris and referred to itself simply as the Situationist International (however I will refer to it as the specto-Situationist International to differentiate it from the original Situationist International and the 2nd Situationist International).

One of the central preoccupations of the Debordist faction of the SI – which after the 1962 split in the movement became the specto-Situationist International – was the idea of 'the overcoming of art'. Debord and the specto-Situationists believed that the possibility of meaningful artistic creation had ceased with dada and surrealism and that the only thing left to be accomplished was the realisation and suppression of 'art'. (See for example thesis 191 of Debord's *Society Of The Spectacle* or Khayati's 'Captive Words' in *Internationale Situationiste* issue 10). Although the specto-Situationist choice of Dada and Surrealism as marking the end of art is not arbitrary – the specto-SI saw itself as the heir to these movements and wanted go 'beyond' their transgression of art – it is incorrect. As we have seen, from a materialist perspective 'art' is a product of capitalist society, therefore – as a practice – it can only become redundant if the bourgeoisie itself is overthrown. The specto-SI believed that capitalism had become decadent at the time of the assault made on it by the first workers movement; Dada and Surrealism being contemporaries of this 'assault' had – so the specto-SI believed – played a similar role in culture to that of proletarian insurgents in the economic and political spheres. The specto-SI see a fundamental break at this point: prior to it both capitalism and its art/culture were progressive, after it they became decadent. My analysis disputes such a view – from a materialist perspective art has never played a progressive role in culture, rather it has served as a justification for snobbery, elitism and oppression since it emerged in its modern form during the eighteenth century.

The specto-Situationists hoped to 'realise and suppress' art through a reinvention of everyday life; the idea was that art would disappear into a poeticised construction of daily existence, to be practised autonomously by a proletarian class who would in effect become 'masters without slaves'. But an aestheticisation of everyday life, and by implication of the proletariat, is in no sense a neutral concept – and such ideas are ultimately the aspirations of an avant-garde fraction within the bourgeois class. Art, poetry – indeed any system of aesthetics that privileges form over content – are ultimately bourgeois concerns. Because the specto-Situationists failed to break with these ideas their practice came to reinforce the overall position of the bourgeoisie. By projecting bourgeois concerns onto the proletariat, the specto-SI made such concerns appear universal (not in the eyes of the working class but for the reassurance of the bourgeoisie). Situationist ideas, emerging as they do from the transgressions of the avant-garde, are alien to – and at war with – popular taste.

The second group we will look at – Fluxus – had, it has been claimed, 'as one of its main focal points the transformation of culture and ideology' (Ken Friedman 'On Fluxus' included in *Flash Art* issue 84/5, October/November 1978). Fluxus hoped to make art more 'democratic'. One of the ways in which this was to be done was through the production of simple scripts that in theory anyone could perform. Two examples by George Brecht from the collection *Water Yam* (Fluxus 1964) are 'Instruction':

'Turn on a radio
At the First sound, turn it off.'

And 'Three Telephone Events':

'When the telephone rings, it is allowed to continue ringing until it stops.
When the telephone rings, the receiver is lifted, then replaced.
When the telephone rings, it is answered.'

While almost anyone is indeed capable of performing these scripts, as soon as one asks the question what sort of person would want to engage in such an activity, it immediately becomes apparent that this 'democratic art' represents the interests of avant-garde elements within the culturally powerful fraction of the bourgeoisie. The Fluxus scripts rely for their impact on their transgression of the norms of bourgeois high culture (a feature characteristic of all avant-garde art) and although simple to perform, the aesthetic system they are based on is at war with popular taste. While bourgeois aesthetes who look for formal innovation in culture – rather than content or 'meaning' – can appreciate such 'democratic' gestures, a proletarian would find the idea that such an activity was worth pursuing ridiculous. Thus although on one level Fluxus scripts invite participation, the intellectual tradition from which such activities have grown is alien to popular taste and inevitably prevents popular participation. Indeed, this class division within culture is drawn upon to authenticate the works of the avant-garde. The popular reaction of derision with which 'avant-garde' work is met is used to reinforce the myth of the artist as an isolated individual in pursuit of progress and humanistic goals (despite the 'difficulties' of having to deal with an 'uncaring' and 'reactionary' public). The fact that the artist, as a part of the dominant class, is able to define what constitutes 'progress' and 'humanism' is conveniently ignored.

The third movement we will look at – the Neoists – were heavily influenced by both the Futurists and Fluxus. The first Neoist group was formed in Montreal in 1979. They were fascinated by video and computers – soft technology was to them what hard technology (motor cars, factories) had been to Marinetti and his circle. Form, in the guise of progress, interested the group far more than content (the implications of technological 'innovations'). The Montreal Neoists were mesmerised by any and every gadget that found its way onto the 'free market'. In this one area their inclinations seem to reflect popular taste. But they combined this with a penchant for avant-garde transgression, that clearly reflects their status as a fraction operating within the ruling class. To give just one example and simultaneously illustrate the group's debt to Fluxus, there is the case of Neoist Istvan Kantor, who began a *Blood Campaign* in 1979 in order to 'raise money for the Neoist Cultural Conspiracy'[1]. Among other things, this consisted of Kantor using his blood to make paintings. Clearly one of the sources that inspired these actions was Yoko Ono's pre-Fluxus 'instruction work' *Blood Piece* (exhibited as part of Ono's first New York show in 1960):

'Use your blood to paint.
a) Keep painting until you faint.
b) Keep painting until you die.'

Such work serves to reinforce all the myths of art and the artist that are so dearly loved by the bourgeoisie – and reproduces ruling class values by privileging form over content, art over life, distance over participation. What is important is not what is depicted (in Kantor's case an abstract mess) but the fact that blood is used as paint.

The Neoists often claimed they were attempting to create 'open situations' in which 'anybody' could participate. But as was the case with Fluxus, mass participation did not occur precisely because the Neoists' stated desire to 'escape from the prison of art' was completely alien to – and at war with – popular taste. The masses do not need to 'escape from the prison of art' because they don't accept the value the bourgeoisie places upon 'cultural capital'.

It is quite likely that most participants in Fluxus and Neoism were absolutely sincere in their desire to make art more 'democratic', just as most Christians are sincere when they pray for the souls of sinners to be saved. Hopefully – through comradely criticism – we can eventually make it clear to those who desire a more 'democratic' art practice, that what is actually needed is the abolition of the capitalist system (and with it the category of art). Specto-situationists and their followers also need pursuading that art should be abolished, but in their case this is rather complicated since in verbal terms they already imagine themselves committed to such a project. What we have to do is convince them that they have not yet fully understood the class basis of culture. As for those who support the present cultural and political system, I have nothing but contempt for these hacks. Meanwhile, the vast majority of ordinary people have the good fortune to stand outside any intellectual argument about the status of art. They understand its class basis intuitively, and have no need of any 'intellectual theory' to reinforce their beliefs (as the popular cry of 'rubbish' in response to avant-garde experimentation demonstrates).

Notes for a lecture at Glasgow Free University 25/3/88

1 It should be noted that Kantor failed to raise money for the 'Neoist Cultural Conspiracy' through the sale of his blood. The use of bodily fluids in 'art works' was already too common by the time Kantor began his 'campaign' in 1979 to create any interest. In the last century, Pre-Raphaelites such as Rossetti had used their sperm as an ingredient in paint making processes. In the late fifties

and early sixties, the nouveaux realiste Manzoni canned his own shit and sold it as an art product. In his 1964 *Meat Show* at Washington Meat Market, Delford Brown made 'liver prints' from animal blood. He also had a nurse draw his blood, a Chinese cook fry it, and then he ate it. To go into other examples of bodily fluids being used in or as 'art works' would be tedious. Similarly, not too much should be made of Kantor's activities in the context of Neoism. The major aim of the 'movement' was the creation of collaborative situations usually involving the consumption of food. Thus no individual should be singled out as being of irreplaceable importance to the group. However, Kiki Bonbon, tentatively a convenience, R. U. Sevol, Pete Horobin, Stiletto, Graf Haufen and John Berndt are among those who played a major role. The author of this text was also briefly involved with the Neoist 'movement'.

Language, identity and the avant-garde

I DO NOT WISH TO BEGIN BY giving an exhaustive definition of 'language'. However, although I intend to concentrate on 'language' in its verbal form, it should be remembered that there are also visual and other types of communication that can be subsumed under the general heading of 'language' – and that such forms are not necessarily 'word' based. Without resorting to 'exhaustive' definitions, it is not possible to demonstrate whether identity can exist autonomously of verbal thought and communication. What I propose to do, is show that under the 'mental sets' of twentieth-century capitalism, the creation of identity is very much dependent upon the manipulation of verbal forms. Specifically I will examine the ways in which the 'avant-garde' manipulates language to form an identity for itself based on appearances of 'rupture', 'difference' and 'refusal'.

When Marinetti wrote *The Founding and First Manifesto of Futurism* in 1909, the Futurist movement didn't exist. Marinetti 'created' the movement by paying for his tract to appear as an advertisement on the front page of the Paris based newspaper *Le Figaro*. Influenced by Sorel's description of the birth of Christianity, Marinetti presented Futurism as an 'absolute' break with the past:

"We stand on the last promontory of the centuries!... Why should we look back, when what we want is to break down the mysterious doors of the Impossible? Time and space died yesterday. We already live in the absolute, because we have created eternal, omnipresent speed.

We will glorify war – the world's only hygiene – militarism, patriotism, the destructive gestures of freedom-bringers, beautiful ideas worth dying for, and scorn for women.

We will destroy the museums, libraries, academies of every kind, will fight moralism, feminism, every opportunistic or utilitarian cowardice."

Marinetti's manifesto was a brilliant piece of rhetoric. It caused a sensation and brought young painters and poets flocking to join the Futurist movement. However, as Ken Hollings notes in 'Art Year Zero' (*Performance* 27, Dec/Jan '84-5): '...the Futurists made no attempt whatsoever to pursue a programme of wholesale destruction of artworks. Subsequent manifestos, either by Marinetti or his followers, made no attempt to deal with this cardinal founding principle, preferring instead to concentrate on issues of form, content and structure, and no major acts of art vandalism by Futurists, individually or collectively have been recorded. A similar disparity between the nihilistic statement and a subsequent lack of action can be found in other European avant-garde movements.'

Marinetti used language to create an aura of destructiveness, and thus controversy, around himself and the Futurist movement. Rhetoric was the means by which an appearance of destructiveness was conjured up; the 'value' of this image was almost entirely symbolic and it had little basis in 'physical reality'. Marinetti played upon the bourgeois fear of violence against property – and as 'theatre', the threat of destruction was titillating to all the classes in western society. If this threat had been turned into a 'physical reality', the Futurists and their activities would have been the subject of severe repression.

(When, on 10 March 1914, the suffragette Mary Richardson attacked a painting housed in the British National Gallery – to protest against the campaign of vilification being carried out against Emily Pankhurst – it came as no surprise that the Futurists did not rally to her cause. Marinetti's verbal attacks upon the artistic ideals of the past were never intended to be taken as anything other than the means for creating a symbolic 'rupture' with entrenched tradition.)

Despite the Futurist's insistence on their own originality, the movement was very much an outgrowth of Romanticism. Futurism clothed itself with aggressive rhetoric in an attempt to obscure the debt it owed to earlier political and artistic formulations. On the level of 'appearance', Marinetti's verbal tirades successfully created a 'cleavage' that 'forced' 'the public' to choose between a Futurist modernity that wished to destroy the oppressive grip of the past over the present and an anaemic academicism which wanted to conserve 'great' western traditions. Thus the Futurists' image as energetic, rebellious and progressive iconoclasts was constructed almost entirely from verbal formulations – the appeal of language being so strong that it proved unnecessary for these claims to be 'backed up' with any form of physical action.

Just as Marinetti owed an often unacknowledged debt to late Romanticism, he inspired other groups – the Vorticists, Dadaists, Surrealists, Lettristes, Situationists, Fluxus, Neoists &c. – who were often unwilling to acknowledge the influence of Futurism on their own activities. The Situationists were, in terms of appearance at least, among the more 'intransigent' of these 'movements'.

Formed in 1957, from the amalgamation of the Lettriste International and the International Movement For An Imaginist Bauhaus, the Situationist International (SI) rarely numbered more than 15 members at any one time. The SI quickly won itself a reputation for sectarianism; at least partly because of its supposedly rigorous criteria for breaks and exclusions from within its own ranks. Those who broke with the movement, or with whom the movement chose to break, were often the subject of public condemnation. However, in private, those who had been condemned often remained on friendly terms with the remaining members of the 'International'. Alexander Trocchi was insistent that he had withdrawn from the SI and had not been – as those with whom he had 'broken' claimed – expelled. Despite this disagreement, he maintained personal contact with individual Situationists for at least another decade. Asger Jorn – nicknamed George Killer after his resignation – went as far as providing the finance for the publication of journals in which he was denounced!

Similarly, despite the fact that many of the concepts and positions it adhered to were contradictory, the SI managed to project an image of 'theoretical coherence'. It did this by way of reference to 'dialectics' and the adoption of a very simple rhetorical trick. The Situationists would present gross generalisation as incontestable fact. If this tactic failed to intimidate those the Situationists had managed to engage in 'dialogue', the group simply resorted to the use of insinuations, insults and lies.

The inadequacies of the Situationists' position on art and the incoherence of the theory of the spectacle have been dealt with elsewhere; they are not worth going into again. Another area in which the SI failed to be theoretically rigorous was in its simultaneous 'rejection' of roles and praise of 'play'. Play is an activity based on the ability to adopt different roles and switch between them – consequently, it is incompatible with the 'rejection' of roles.

In their image building rhetoric, the Situationists went so far as to claim that there was no such thing as 'situationism' ('The notion of situationism is obviously derived by anti-Situationists' – *Internationale Situationiste* issue 1). If the SI had been serious about its claim that it rejected roles, this position would have been reversed. (i.e. 'There is no such thing as a Situationist; there is only Situationism, a doctrine that rejects the adoption – on both an individual and group level – of identities and roles'). However, the Situationists preferred the image of coherence to coherence itself. They used Hegel-speak to dress themselves in the 'anti-role' of 'militant revolutionaries'. Despite this, the SI wasn't interested in revolution, it simply used language to create an identity for its members as 'intransigent communitarians'.

Since the history of the avant-garde is more or less a history of the creation of identities realised through the manipulation of language, the PRAXIS group has suggested that there should be a three year 'Refusal Of Creativity' between 1990 and 1993. During this period, artists and politicos should refrain from engaging in any verbal or physical activities which reinforce their 'difference' – that is to say actions and formulations from which artistic or political identities could be sustained. PRAXIS do not suggest that it is possible to abandon 'roles' altogether. Rather they see it as desirable to switch between various existing roles, to prevent 'character armour' from hardening. If our identities are – at least partially – formed through language, then they are far from immutable…

Aesthetics and resistance

Totality reconsidered

I'D LIKE TO BEGIN BY ADDRESSING THE QUESTION as to why there is currently a massive revival of interest in the activities of avant-garde groups of the fifties and sixties such as the Situationists and Fluxus. There are a number of interrelated reasons for this interest:

Now that post-modernism is no longer fashionable, many people find themselves attracted to the iconoclasm and sense of purpose offered in the work and ideas of the Situationists, Fluxus &c. Support for this work is in part a reaction to the emphasis on the loss of meaning, the proliferation of margins and the decentred subject within post-modern discourse.

Related to the iconoclasm of these groups is the aura of radicality (and by inference authenticity) that surrounds them. Since much academic discourse is grounded in notions of the authentic (and its loss), individuals engaged in cultural and media studies find the prospect of assimilating the 'radicality' attached to 'avant-garde' ideas a very attractive proposition. The book *Recodings: Art, Spectacle, Cultural Politics* by Hal Foster, in which a bastardised version of specto-Situationist theory is wielded in defence of blue-chip art may be taken as a typical example of this trend.

As Colin Gleadell notes in the June '89 issue of *Art Monthly*: 'As more collectors seeking major works turn from the thin pickings on the Old Master market or from the astronomical costs involved in Impressionist and modern paintings, post-war and contemporary art seem to offer the greater potential.' The Situationists and Fluxus have been caught up in this process and as the prices paid for paintings, objects and publications rise, there is an accompanying increase in publicity – much of it stimulated and/or financed by the collectors and dealers trading in the work of these groups.

It has become something of a tradition that early commentaries historifying avant-garde groups should be produced by individuals who actively participated in the events they later eulogise (cf. *En Avant Dada: A History*

Of Dadaism and *Dada Lives* by Richard Huelsenbeck – and Ken Friedman's commentaries on Fluxus). In the case of the Situationists, the form of this historification has been particularly biased due to Guy Debord gaining the patronage of Gerald Lebovici. Among other things, Lebovici's money financed the publishing house Champ Libre which disseminated propaganda advertising Debord's supposedly intransigent lifestyle.

Before addressing the issue of recuperation, I'd like repeat two observations that have been made about the Situationists.

1 Writing in *Here and Now* #6/7 (Spring 1989), Gus MacDonald suggests that 'Debord's *Society of the Spectacle* is a perfect art object for a specialised audience, complete with homage, pastiche and reference to tradition, designed for the contemplative pleasure of its formalistic perfection.'

2 As Laura Romild and Jacques Vincent note in *Echecs Situationistes* (Paris 1988), the keystone of the Debordist myth is the famous appeal for a general occupation strike and the formation of workers' councils published by the first Sorbonne Occupation Committee, with specto-Situationist participation, on 16th May 1968. However, what Debord's supporters tend to overlook is that the appeal, coming after the start of the strikes, had no effect on the unfolding of events! And so, while the specto-Situationists have always claimed they played a major role in the May events and cited them as a vindication of their theory, any informed and objective observer is unlikely to take such assertions seriously.

In view of this, I would suggest there is no question of specto-Situationist ideas having been recuperated by a 'spectacular' (or indeed any other sort of) society. To suggest that Situationist theory has been hijacked by the capitalist media is to credit the former with a critical rigour it did not achieve and the latter with a totalising power it does not possess. It's manipulation, and not recuperation, when those with a vested interest in the status quo make claims about the Situationists having produced the total revolutionary critique. If we take onboard such disabling beliefs then we could well end up living out one of the ideologies created by our parents generation – and if we accept that the Situationists not only created the total revolutionary critique but that this critique has been recuperated, then we resign ourselves to whatever fate society allots us.

Notes made for a panel discussion held at the Institute Of Contemporary Arts, London 24/6/89

Part 2

From Dialectics to Stasis

Ruins of Glamour/ Glamour of Ruins

FOR THOSE OF YOU WITH SHORT MEMORIES, or who were unable to attend the exhibition, I will run through its artists and detail some of their exhibits. Stefan Szczelkun's felt covered and smoke belching wendy house was not simply a post-modern pastiche of Joseph Beuys, it was also a means of making the viewer re-evaluate their attitude towards childhood. Hannah Vowles and Glyn Banks burnt their work not simply as an episode in the reinvention of Fluxus and Auto-Destructive Art, but also to demonstrate the role of destruction in the construction of glamour. Rather than losing their glamorous appeal, the burnt paintings actually 'appeared' more glamorous as a result of their incineration. Stewart Home presented a huge wall painting of a junkie shooting up, with the intention of revealing the role of the glamorous victim in the social (re)production of Power. Tom McGlynn came from New York to present to an English audience his demolition of the appearance of glamour in consumer society. He did this with an exact scale enlargement of a calf from a children's farm yard toy set. The heroism and glamour of the increased size was nullified by the magnification of the numerous flaws pre-existing in the piece of plastic junk McGlynn used as his model. Ed Baxter, Andy Hopton and Simon Dickason, used spiked sculpture as a metaphor for the links between glamour, violence and destruction. Gabrielle Quinn explored the ethereal glamour of decay with an installation of decomposing heads. Rick Gibson served visitors to the show with food and wine, while wearing a see-through plastic vest lined with living worms. This performance was intended to bring to mind a very literal anal/ogy between glamour and corruption. And to really ram home the message that glamour can be, and is, constructed from the ugliest of materials, the most nihilistic of urges, the floor of the gallery was lined with coke. This last gesture was bitterly ironic, contrasting as it did the heat and history implied by the fossilised fuel to the 'cool' atmosphere pervading both glamour and the under-heated gallery.

Thus if glamour is usually viewed as a 'desirable' given, the *Ruins of Glamour/Glamour of Ruins* show can be seen as a continuous performance in which 'artists', objects and audience, endlessly deconstruct and reconstruct 'glamour' – a process that eventually results in the exposure of the mechanisms underpinning this oppressive reification.

Ruins of Glamour/Glamour of Ruins

Chisenhale Studios, London December 1986

Desire in Ruins:

statement

1 *Desire In Ruins*, like *Ruins of Glamour/Glamour of Ruins*, seeks the negation of all forms of abstraction. It contests the myths of individuality and value built on contemporary art practice. Indeed, it contests art practice itself. Thus the installation stands in opposition to both modernism AND post-modernism, which are simply two stages in a single trajectory.

2 Like *Ruins of Glamour*, *Desire In Ruins* exposes the control mechanisms built into architecture. The wall pieces in these 'shows' trigger in the 'spectator' a standard response to the gallery as an architectural space in which art is displayed. The gallery acts as a frame within which one set of 'ideas' and 'experiences' are sealed off from all others and, as a direct result of this separation, granted a privileged position. By 'unconventional' deployment of floor pieces and lighting, *Desire In Ruins* interrupts the smooth-running of this function and reveals the ideological role played by all systems of value.

3 A brief description of *Ruins of Glamour* may assist orientation to *Desire In Ruins*. Spectators entering Chisenhale Studios, London, during the course of the *Glamour* show, found themselves blinded by a spotlight. Since there was a wall to their left, they were forced to veer right. They thus found themselves entering a spiral of heaped coal. Any progression beyond the outer ring of the spiral was impeded by sharpened wood spikes. Similarly, it was not possible to step over the spiral at the point where the spotlight was hung. Spectators were forced to step over the spiral at a point just in front of the spotlight. By turning their backs to the light, they found themselves at the best vantage point for viewing both the exhibition and any other spectators (particularly those entering the gallery).

Desire In Ruins – Transmission Gallery, Glasgow May 1987

The role of sight in recent cultural history

THE TEXT IS A STAGE OF THE SPECTACLE, and the Spectacle is fully realised in the text.

Text is 'vision' for those who cannot see. It 'explains' the world in terms that render its very 'explanations' 'meaningless'. More real than the real, text seeks to illuminate the world with a light so intense it will irreparably damage the retina, leaving the 'reader' in a position where s/he, too, can no longer see.

Text is 'inner vision', 'insight', a 'powerful device' that denies the 'reality' of Power. Words, a series of ciphers strung across the physical space of a page, letters arranged to create 'meanings'. This final characteristic is totally at odds with the avowed 'tenets' of the 'post-modern scene'. Ironically, the concept of hyperreality has been articulated almost 'exclusively' through the manipulation of text.

The 'crisis of the sign' doesn't exist outside the confines of the university and the salon. Post-modernism serves Capital precisely because it promotes a debate over 'meaning'. What interests those in Power is the effect (use value) of symbols, both singularly and in combination. Thus while 'post-modernists' rant about the 'loss of the real', advertising agencies continue to sell products by effectively manipulating signs.

If post-modernism was taken to its 'logical' conclusion, 'art' would be indistinguishable from 'advertising'. Instead, 'art marketeers' package the manipulation of pre-existing language by 'fine artists' as a 'new' art practice. Thus the shift from 'modernism' to 'post-modernism' consists of a switch from (deliberately) failed attempts to create a 'new' and 'universal' language, to an admission that art is utterly bankrupt.

Desire In Ruins – Transmission Gallery, Glasgow May 87

Plagiarism as negation in culture

GIVEN THE TOTAL COLONISATION OF daily life by Capital, we are forced to speak the received language of the media. It has always been impossible to give coherent expression to thoughts and practices that oppose the dominant ideology. However, we do not seek the creation of new languages. Such an act is doomed to failure and plays into Capital's hands (by reinforcing the myths of 'originality' and 'individual creativity'). Rather, we aim to reinvent the language of those who would control us.

While we refute the concept of 'originality', we do not find it problematic that the idea of plagiarism implies an original. Although we believe all 'human creativity' is accumulative (that is to say that all 'innovations' are built on the sum total of what has gone before), it does not trouble us that there is, in the past, a 'point of origin'. We cannot give an account of this 'point of origin' and will not waste our time making philosophical speculations about such irrelevancies.

Plagiarism is the negative point of a culture that finds its ideological justification in the 'unique'. Indeed, it is only through the creation of unique identities that commodification can take place. Thus the unsuccessful search for a new and universal language by 'modernist' artists should be viewed as a high point of the capitalist project. However, this in no way implies that 'post-modernism' is somehow more 'radical' than its precursor. Both movements were simply stages in a single trajectory. Such developments reflect the establishment's ability to recuperate actions and concepts that in the past threatened its very constitution. 'Post-modern appropriation' is very different to plagiarism. While post-modern theory asserts that there is no longer any basic reality, the plagiarist recognises that Power is always a reality in historical society.

Post-modernists fall into two categories. The first of these are cynics who understand the ideological process in which they play a minor role and manipulate the system for personal gain. The second category of post-modernists are simply naive. Bombarded by media images, they believe that the ever changing 'normality' presented by the press and tv, constitutes a loss of 'reality'. The plagiarist, by contrast, recognises the role the media plays in masking the mechanisms of Power, and actively seeks to disrupt this function.

By reconstituting dominant images, by subjectivising them, we aim to create a 'normality' better suited to our requirements than the media nightmare dictated by Power. However, we have never imagined that this can be achieved solely through 'gallery' exposure. The images used to sell washing powder have a powerful hold over our consciousness precisely because these clichés are so often reproduced in the media. For an image to be effective it needs continuous reproduction in the press and on tv. The only viable alternative to our strategy of exposure to images reconstituted by the process of plagiarism, is the physical destruction of transmission stations and print technology.

Desire In Ruins – Transmission Gallery, Glasgow May 87

Plagiarism

PLAGIARISM IS THE CONSCIOUS MANIPULATION of pre-existing elements in the creation of 'aesthetic' works. Plagiarism is inherent in all 'artistic' activity, since both pictorial and literary 'arts' function with an inherited language, even when their practitioners aim at overthrowing this received syntax (as happened with modernism and post-modernism).

At the beginning of the twentieth-century, the way in which pre-existing elements were used in 'artistic' productions underwent a quantitative leap with the discovery of collage. This development was pre-figured in the 'writings' of Isidore Ducasse (1846-70), who is better known by his pen name Lautreamont.

In his Poems, Ducasse wrote: 'Plagiarism is necessary. Progress implies it'. This maxim summarises the use to which plagiarism has been put ever since. Two, or more, divergent elements are brought together to create new meanings. The resulting sum is greater than the individual parts.

The Lettristes, and later the Situationists, called this process 'detournement' (diversion is a literal translation from the French), but the activity is still popularly known as plagiarism – the term that Lautreamont used.

Plagiarism enriches human language. It is a collective undertaking far removed from the post-modern 'theories' of appropriation. Plagiarism implies a sense of history and leads to progressive social transformation. In contrast, the 'appropriations' of post-modern ideologists are individualistic and alienated. Plagiarism is for life, post-modernism is fixated on death.

Festival of Plagiarism – London January/February 1988

Multiple names

MULTIPLE NAMES ARE 'TAGS' that the avant-garde of the seventies and eighties proposed for serial use. They have taken a number of forms, but are more commonly 'invented personal names' which, their proponents claim, anyone can take on as a 'context' or 'identity'. The idea is usually to create a collective body of artistic works using the 'invented identity'.

The first of these 'collective identities', 'Klaos Oldanburg', was propagated by the British mail artists Stefan Kukowski and Adam Czarnowski in the mid-seventies. A few years later, the American mail artist, David Zack, proposed 'Monty Cantsin' as the name of the 'first open pop-star', a name anybody could use. Factional differences between those using the 'Monty Cantsin' tag resulted in the 'rival' names of 'No Cantsin' and 'Karen Eliot', both of which emerged in the mid-eighties. A number of individuals and groups have independently 'originated' similar concepts. For example, a group centred around Sam Durrant in Boston (USA) proposed 'Bob Jones' as a multiple identity in the mid-eighties.

There have been multiple names for magazines ('Smile' originating in England in 1984) and pop groups ('White Colours' first proposed in England in 1982).

Multiple names are connected to radical theories of play. The idea is to create an 'open situation' for which no one in particular is responsible. Some proponents of the concept also claim that it is a way to 'practically examine, and break down, western philosophic notions of identity, individuality, value and truth'.

Festival of Plagiarism – London January/February 1988

Soon...

DESPITE ITS OBVIOUS FUNCTION AS a guide to the *Anon* installation, the present text has not been composed with the intention of attaching a fixed meaning to the exhibition.

Anon has been installed with a view to disrupting those productive and administrative procedures that tend to reduce the role of the audience (at least in terms of appearance) to that of passive spectators.

The title of the show is an indication of the participants' wish to question the status granted to the so called 'creator' in the production of culture. However, despite the title, it would have been counter-productive for those participating in the exhibition to remain 'completely anonymous', since this would result in undue attention being focused upon their possible identities (cf. The Residents). Thus while our names have not been given 'headline' status (for example by placing them on the invitation card for the 'private view'), we haven't made any great secret of 'who we are'.

A number of tactics have been employed in an attempt to prevent those individuals stunted by laziness and vested interest from adopting a purely contemplative attitude towards the installation. Upon entering the gallery, visitors find themselves under a spotlight and in front of a reception desk. To proceed, one must turn right. The intention here is to reinforce (by analogy) a conscious awareness of how town planners, architects and others, seek to predetermine our movement within the urban environment; simultaneously, it is intended to provoke a critical response to the 'art space' as a site of Power.

While Power always flows in two directions, there is a great deal to be done before such flows are brought into a state of equilibrium. Within the realm of 'the arts', a general recognition of the productive role played by the audience in the creation of culture would go a long way towards curbing the snobbery and elitism that is endemic throughout the contemporary cultural scene.

Anon – 33 Arts Centre, Luton February/March 1989

A short rant concerning our 'Cultural Condition'

WITH THE REDUCTION OF PUBLIC SPENDING on culture, it is possible – particularly in more 'experimental' fields – for 'autonomous' elements to destroy the hegemony of the bland initiatives favoured by grant dispensing bodies. In particular areas – which will never be 'financially viable' or 'attractive' to business sponsors – grant cutting, which monetarists imagine delivers culture to the 'free market' (as though culture were no more than a superstructural effect of the economy!), actually offers control of entire sectors of the arts to those whose hatred of capitalism is the most fanatical (and who are quite prepared to 'work' without any financial 'reward').

A major component of such 'fanaticism' is the refusal to make universalist claims for any form of cultural production (and to mock these and similar assertions that artists have traditionally used to 'justify' their work). A genuinely 'radical' cultural practice must reject essentialism and simultaneously recognise the reality of the Power relationships that characterise our society. (Post-modernists reject essentialism in theory while simultaneously exploiting the humanist ideology of 'romantic' and 'modernist' art whose legacy enables them to receive grants and enjoy state financed teaching careers. On the subject of what characterises this society, these nouveaux Nietzscheans – or at least the Baudrillardian wing of this 'movement' – make the completely ridiculous claim that Power has 'disappeared').

However, the aforesaid should not be mistaken for some form of neo-Marxism – although capitalist society is characterised by gross inequalities of Power, there is (at present) no unified class in the process of carrying through a collective programme to transform social relations (nor is there any historic 'inevitability' that such a class formation will appear in the foreseeable future). For these reasons, I have adopted a strategy of struggle – here and now – in an area which is of immediate concern to me (rather than attempting to 'organise the class' or act as 'a torch of enlightenment' to others). In any case, organisation along the lines of 'new social movements' seems eminently more sensible than attempting to impose traditional Marxian class models on a society that has undergone enormous changes since these were first outlined (and even 150 years ago such models were worse than useless since any 'genuine' understanding of class requires more than mere economic reductionism).

The Marxist-Leninist assertion that human society consists of an economic base and a cultural and political superstructure is utter nonsense; there is a dynamic interaction between economics, culture and politics (any of these categories may assume dominance at a specific time according to the interplay of historical factors). An analogous pattern of interaction exists between production and consumption (since the onset of industrialisation neither of these two categories has enjoyed a state of permanent dominance over the other). Hence my concern to emphasise the productive role played by the audience in the cultural sphere. Concomitant with this concern is a rejection of the idea that there is a 'radical and politicised body of semi-passive consumers' eagerly awaiting the opportunity to attend events such as the Anon installation (and it is for this reason that I have seized upon the opportunity to site work in locations where it will be seen by individuals who have not planned to view it – i.e. the display units located in Luton shopping centre).

Anon – 33 Arts Centre, Luton February/March 1989

Part 3

Neoist Reprise

Neoist correspondence script

15/4/84 Woking, England.
Dear Neoist Persons
I am a young person whose interest was very much captured by the photo and short piece about APT 8 in the latest issue of *Performance* magazine. Could you please zap me back some info. in the SAE I've enclosed.
As Above
So Below
Monty Cantsin.

17/4/84 London, England.
Monty Cantsin
We Neoists are deeply involved with vegetables and chapatis. The only concrete data on APT 8 is enclosed. I suggest you come here at 20.00 hours this Saturday evening for a live exchange. You can meet us and discuss your future participation.
Cantsin and Cantsin.

16/5/84 Immortality Center, Mexico.
Hmm, Cantsin, friends call you Monty. I have lots of material on Monty Cantsin since I made up the name and sent it on a postcard to Cantsin. I'm doing hmm, this filing project where I put all my correspondence material in these correspondence novels. So now Cantsin is in Monty Cantsin's Cell system. An emerging novel. So I'll put you in with Monty Cantsin RAF VEC and you can be Monty Cantsin in that book if you want.
Monty Cantsin.

11/6/84 Winnipeg, Canada.
Dearest friend, I arrived here yesterday, it's a Neoist city with the red river

and the golden boy atop the dome of the Manitoba legislative building. Your immortal friend,
Cantsin.

15/6/84 Regina, Canada.
Dearest friend, Monty Cantsin was living in this prairie city for ten years. He came to Budapest from Regina in 1976. Indians here are fat and alcoholists. I drew some blood for them last night. United Cells of Neoism,
Cantsin.

18/6/84 Calgary, Canada.
Dearest conspirator, I am getting closer to the Athabasca glacier and ready for the meeting with Monty Cantsin. Your immortal friend,
Cantsin.

22/6/84 Calgary, Canada.
Dearest friend, I met Monty Cantsin on the Athabasca glazier. He drew my blood and he turned into gold. I took his gold bust. It looks like me. My mission is accomplished. Your immortal friend,
Cantsin.

23/6/84 Immortality Center, Mexico.
Hmm, Monty Cantsin, I am Monty Cantsin. I have to tell you there is no problem, more like a project. OK. Who can say what the whole thing is.
Monty Cantsin.

7/7/84 Neoist Embassy, Montreal, Canada.
Dear Monty, yes it was long but I did it, met Monty Cantsin. Now I get ready for new adventures. Bread expedition, ah? And what about bread ballet? Your immortal friend,
Monty Cantsin.

26/7/84 Data Cell, Dysart, Scotland.
Monty, pram goes on the road Saturday 28/7/84. Please deliver enclosed envelope to Monty Cantsin. Travel broadens the myth. See you in Lumsden.
Monty.

August 84 Crater Bal Tim Ore, USA.

Dear Monty, thanks for the cell stamp. Info., my depression deepens, much thought of suicide, no money, my correspondence declines. More later if I live.
Monty Cantsin.

6/8/84 Berlin, Germany.

Dear Mr. Cantsin. Monty Cantsin. Smiling Monty Cantsin. &c. I'm Monty Cantsin. I have a fine correspondence with Monty Cantsin since awhile (but short in relation to my use of mail art since five years). I saw your name mentioned on his papers sent to me occasionally and I already knew the outline of the Monty Cantsin image since awhile. From Monty Cantsin publication too I heard of Neoist sometimes. So let me say that if it is possible I want to speak with the author of the images – Cantsin, if I get it all together in the right way. And in the sense that I would like to use your personal name. Your surname that I don't know. I hope there is nothing hurting in this reflection for you. Maybe it's your concept to work with this.
Monty Cantsin.

9/8/84 Neoist Embassy, Montreal, Canada.

Dear Cantsin, I'm the black light in the pure white colours and my blood keeps flowing, flowing. It was nice to see you and talk about revolution. I want to die in the tv. Your immortal friend,
Cantsin.

6/9/84 Neoist Embassy, Montreal, Canada.

Dear Cantsin, every five minutes we need a new solution, we are alive and do our best for total freedom. Get ready for the next six years. Oh yes, in the blue endless skies a flaming iron flies. The record is out very soon. *Mass Media*. Every five minutes we need a new robot and more more more. More Monty Cantsin and Six Finger Club and more *Smile*. More more more. Every five minutes we must eat a brain. Your immortal friend,
Monty

September 84 San Antonio, Texas.

Dear Monty, or Cantsin if you prefer. Monty (or maybe he's not calling himself that now?!). I remember once in Portland Oregon he went around

for several days calling himself Christ and going toot toot but this turned out to be the botulism he'd contracted from Cantsin's clams casino surprise which surprised all of us who'd eaten it. I myself went around for several days thinking my hair had turned white overnight when in reality it had all fallen out.
Cantsin.

9/11/84 Beograd, Yugoslavia.
Dear Monty Cantsin or Christ or Son of God. OK, who are you, or are you who? If you're Monty Cantsin, you must remind our meeting at Monty Cantsin's home, later at my home. We did a performance video show at my home (*Blood Is Gold*). Next days I organised big mixed media programme and exhibition called *World's Artists Family* at the Beograd Cultural Centre Gallery. Best wishes,
Monty Cantsin.

20/11/84 Eugene, Oregon, USA.
Dear Monty or Christ. Are you the same Monty Cantsin who came here to Eugene in 1979 and painted yer moustache red with poster paint and came to the big party we held and the FOAMLORDS, then a fledgling failure played? I don't think you are actually. I think that you're an impostor. Don't laugh, I know! I got pretty much to be Monty Cantsin for awhile there myself. Anyway, he was an OK kinda guy so I figure any Monty Cantsin is OK by me. The Monty Cantsin fellow was from Czechoslovakia or somewhere and watched me have sex with my girlfriend on the floor. Fortunately it was my girlfriend and my floor.
Monty Cantsin.

24/11/84 Crater Baltimore, USA.
Monty, the concept of Monty Cantsin. Monty Cantsin is a name chosen/invented by Monty Cantsin to refer to an international star who can be anyone. The name is fixed, the people using it aren't.
Monty Cantsin.

Retro-Futurism

JAMES SENIOR GLANCED AT HIS WATCH as he strode out of Kennington tube station. It was seven twenty-two. He was expected for supper at eight. James had not met the people he was going to dine with. He did not even know how many of them there would be. He was going to meet the organisers of the Eighth International Neoist Apartment Festival. James was not sure what Neoism was. A friend had written urging him to get in touch with the people organising the Neoist Festival in London. James had sent a letter to the address supplied by his friend and four days later, he'd received a reply inviting him to supper on 12 May.

James pulled a London street map from his bag. He was standing on Kennington Park Road. All he had to do was cross the road, walk in the direction of Kennington Park until he came to Ravensdown Street, turn left off Ravensdown onto Stannary Street and then right into Aulton Place. This took four minutes. Number thirteen was easy to spot because it had a large sign planted in the front garden on which the word NEOISM was crudely painted in block capitals. James was rather disappointed to discover Aulton Place consisted simply of rotting two up, two downs, with no more than a paved street separating the terrace from a towering factory wall. Several of the houses were derelict, with their windows smashed and their roofs missing. None of the occupied homes looked as though they could have met official housing standards.

James checked his watch, he was early. He walked back onto Kennington Park Road. It was a busy street with shabby shops and several pubs scattered amongst the grimy flats and houses. He strolled towards the Elephant and Castle, then turned around and headed back to Aulton Place. James passed an attractive girl, he turned his head and caught her glancing back at him. For a moment their eyes met, then each turned away and continued walking in opposite directions. James felt ridiculous. He wished he'd had the courage to say something. He crossed the road and walked into Kennington Park. It didn't take him long to find a public toilet, where he urinated before hurrying out.

James checked his watch again upon reaching Aulton Place and discovered he still had time to kill. He stood on the street comer for a couple of minutes, then marched smartly up to number thirteen and knocked authoritively on the door. There was no bell or knocker, he'd rapped with his knuckles. After a thirty second pause, he knocked again. James could hear someone stomping down the stairs. A woman of about thirty opened the door. She was slightly smaller than James, more heavily built with blue eyes and bleached hair.

'I'm James Senior.'

'Hi, come in, I'm Judy Shaw,' the woman drawled in an American accent.

James offered her his hand, she clasped it firmly.

'Come upstairs, Mark hasn't finished cooking yet, we can relax in my room.'

Judy led James into a room littered with magazines and papers.

'You said in your letter you'd been doing mail art.'

'Yes.'

'What sort of things?'

'Postcards, collage, xerox, a lot with rubber stamps, junk mail.'

'Done any performance?'

'No, I'd like to,' James wasn't sure whether he really believed what he'd just said

'What we're attempting to do with this Apartment Festival,' Judy drawled, 'is create an open situation in which anyone can participate. We're trying to remove the barriers between artist and audience, to abolish the separation between the production and consumption of the art experience.'

'I see,' James said although he'd not understood a word that Judy uttered.

'Ultimately, we believe that the only art work really worth producing is your own life.'

'Yes,' James replied, he was wondering when supper would be ready.

'And so we've replaced the word artist with the term Neoist. Neoism describes the total human being – someone who lives a fully integrated life, someone who regards cooking and making love as greater aesthetic experiences than painting or sculpture.'

James wondered how much longer Judy would ramble on.

'Neoism calls for the world to be adapted to wo/man, rather than having wo/man adapt to the world. It heralds a new era of history, the death of history itself...'

James was relieved to hear a knock on the bedroom door.

'Come in,' sighed Judy.

'Supper's ready,' announced a slightly built man in his mid-thirties.

'Mark, this is James Senior. James, this is Mark West,' Judy said, introducing the two men.

James and Mark shook hands.

'Hello,' Mark said.

'Hello.' echoed James.

As James allowed his hand to drop, Mark removed a note book and pencil from a breast pocket. The older man glanced at his watch and made a note in the book.

'Shall we go through to the kitchen?' Mark made the words sound like a command rather than a question.

Already seated at a wooden table was a twenty-eight year old woman. Hazel Jones had bleached hair and a fiery look in her eye, she was introduced as Mark's girlfriend.

Dinner was a vegetable casserole served with chapattis, a side salad and large quantities of white wine. Once James began eating, Mark explained how he got up at six-thirty every morning to steal vegetables from the bins at New Covent Garden Market. Judy made no attempt to disguise her boredom at hearing this tale repeated yet again.

'Do you make a living from your art?' James asked Mark.

'I'm a full time artist, I support myself on the social.'

'You're a performance artist?'

'I do some performance, mainly I collect data.'

'What kind of data?'

'All kinds.'

'Is that what the note book's for?'

'Yes, I record as much as I can. The times I get up, go to bed, depart from somewhere and arrive somewhere else, the name of anyone I meet and the time at which I meet them, what and when I eat and drink, the times at which I piss and crap, the times at which I have sex and how long it takes me to reach orgasm.'

'I see,' James replied, 'and what do you do with all this data?'

'I put it into data books.'

'And what do you do with these data books?'

'I sell them when I can to museums and collectors.'

Once the dishes had been cleared away, Hazel pulled a bottle of vodka from a bag.

'I thought we might need this,' she said.

By the time the vodka was finished, James was extremely drunk. Mark and Hazel had gone to bed, James was alone with Judy.

'What are we going to do with you?' Judy asked rhetorically. 'You don't look like you'll make it home. There's a mattress in the room beneath mine – or if you prefer, you can sleep with me.'

'I'll sleep with you.'

WHEN JAMES AWOKE HE FELT SICK. Judy was still asleep. James wasn't sure how he should behave and so he just lay where he was. Judy woke up. James pretended to be asleep. Judy got out of bed. James turned over and groaned.

'I'm going to see some people,' Judy announced as she was dressing. 'I'll be back around three. Stay if you like, if you don't, then come back soon. We'll work on that performance we talked about last night.'

James groaned in assent. Judy kissed the back of his neck.

'You're such a baby.'

James smiled into the pillow. He wasn't sure how long it was before he got up. Judy was gone, the house was empty. James drank a glass of water and left.

JAMES LOOKED OUT OF HIS WINDOW but didn't take in what he saw. He decided to go back to bed. He'd spent the best part of two days asleep. When he awoke it was dark. He dressed without putting the light on, left his room and walked down through Whitechapel to Tower Bridge and the Thames.

JAMES WASN'T SURE HOW HE'D ARRIVED in Kennington. At a little after six in the morning, he found himself sitting in the garden of 13 Aulton Place. Thirty minutes later Mark emerged from the house.

'Hello,' said Mark, unsuccessfully attempting to hide his surprise.

'Hello,' echoed James.

'Coming to steal vegetables?'

'Yes,' answered James.

Mark made an entry in his note book and the two men marched off in silence. It didn't take long to get to the market. James watched as Mark pulled discarded vegetables from bins, examined them – and if they were edible, put them in his carrier. When he'd filled the bag, Mark pulled a second carrier from his pocket. There were quite a number of people collecting vegetables., picking up what had been thrown away by the traders. They seemed to be a permanent feature of the market, the security men simply ignored them despite the fact that technically they were committing theft.

Back at Aulton Place, Mark sat James down and put a cup of tea in front of him. James watched Mark stack the vegetables in a cupboard beneath the sink. Once he'd completed this task, Mark left the kitchen, then returned a couple of minutes later with a bundle of papers.

'You were too drunk to take these the other night, they'll interest you, they're about Neoism.'

'Thanks.'

'I'm going out now. It'll be some time before Judy gets up but you've got something to read, you'll be alright.'

JUDY GOT UP AT NOON, she popped her head around the kitchen door on her way to the bathroom.

'Hi, I'm glad you've come. I'll wash, dress and be with you.'

She returned forty minutes later.

'Hi,' Judy said.

'Hi,' echoed James.

'How are you?'

'Fine.'

'Good, would you like something to eat?'

'Yes.' James replied.

Judy cooked bacon and eggs, she liked English breakfasts but gave most of the food to James.

'I'm going to sit in the park. Are you coming?' Judy asked.

'Yes,' replied James, not convinced that he wanted to sit in the park.

JAMES WOKE AT NINE and immediately decided he wanted to see Judy. He walked, if he'd taken the tube he'd have arrived far too early. James knocked on the door. No response. He knocked again. No response. He knocked even harder. No one was home. James went and sat in Kennington Park. An hour later, he went back to number thirteen. Mark answered the door.

'Hello, come in, Judy's out with a couple of her friends. They arrived last night, they flew in from New York.'

Mark sat James down in the kitchen and put a cup of tea in front of him. Judy didn't come home until well after dark. With her were the conceptual artist Person Person and his blind lover Birgit Smith. Person had adopted his rather curious moniker because he felt traditional names reeked of a romantic individualism that any serious artist should abandon. He always introduced Birgit as his blind lover – it would have been more accurate to describe her as partially sighted. Person and Birgit were tired, after tea and chapattis they went to bed.

'I've had an idea about a performance we could do,' Judy announced.

'Yes,' replied James.

'We stand facing each other, while simultaneously chanting our given name and taking off our clothes. Then I put on your clothes and you put on my clothes, while we chant each others name.'

'I'd prefer something a bit more static,' James replied.

He was horrified by the idea of being seen naked in public.

'Oh, come on, don't tell me you're shy!'

'I don't know, I'll think about it.'

JAMES WAS WOKEN AT SIX-THIRTY by the sound of footsteps echoing through the house. He got up. Judy turned over and went back to sleep. Peter Murray had just arrived from Edinburgh on the over-night train, Mark and Hazel were helping him carry his bags up the stairs.

By seven, James, Mark, Peter and Hazel were sitting round the kitchen table enjoying a communal breakfast of muesli, toast and black coffee. Mark and Peter were old friends, their intimacy left James and Hazel feeling like intruders. Hazel decided to go home, James said he'd walk her to the bus stop.

Hazel guided James down to the Oval, from where she'd catch a bus to East Dulwich.

'You seeing Judy?'

'Yeah.'

'Don't you think she's a little old for you?'

'I don't know.'

JUDY GOT UP REASONABLY EARLY by her standards – about eleven-thirty. Once she'd washed, Judy made a breakfast of boiled eggs. It was the second meal James had eaten that day.

'Have you thought about whether you'll do the performance?'

'Yes.'

'And?'

'I'll do it.'

Judy beamed, James smiled. He hadn't decided whether he'd really go through with the performance but James knew that by saying he'd do it, he'd make Judy happy. She leaned across the table and kissed him.

When they'd finished eating, Judy suggested they go and sit in Kennington Park.

WHEN JAMES ARRIVED AT AULTON PLACE, he found Jurgen Braun constructing a Neoist Altar in the street outside number thirteen. Judy had told James a great deal about Jurgen, and James recognised this world class performance artist by his attire – a red coat, gold shoes and a brown and gold rain hat.

The front door was open and James walked into the hall where he found Mark sticking pieces of mail art to the walls. Mark had spent the best part of the day constructing a data installation in his room and was now making the final touches to the house before the opening ceremony of the Neoist Festival later that evening. One of these touches was that everything in number thirteen had a name card attached to it. The walls had cards saying 'wall' tacked to them, tables had cards saying 'table' tacked to them, doors had cards saying 'door' tacked to them – and so on, so that virtually every object in the house had a neatly written card tacked to it, stating exactly what it was.

Upstairs, James ran into Gloria Swann, a professional model and part time performance artist from the States. Judy had slipped out of her usual jeans and T-shirt and was clad in a black cat-suit. She was carefully applying one of several successive layers of make-up to her face.

Terry Wood, a twenty-year old mail artist was hanging model aircraft from the kitchen ceiling. Time ticked inexorably away, bringing the

Flaming Chapatti Opening ever nearer. Marianne Greenwood, Braun's girlfriend, emerged from the basement. She refused to speak so much as a word to anyone but Jurgen – but silently accepted any food she was offered.

Brett Johnson arrived with his entourage – his boyfriend Adrian Foster and a teenager named Charles White, who'd been seduced into attending the Neoist Festival with promises of art world fame. Hazel appeared, she'd brought along a friend of hers called John. Person Person, Birgit Smith and Peter Murray emerged from the sanctuary of their beds. Karl Pratt, a performance artist from Northern Ireland, failed miserably in his attempt to make an impression as he entered the kitchen. His fellow Irishmen, Kevin Alderman and the poet Stephen Brady came in behind him.

Mark ushered everyone from the kitchen and into the street, announcing that Jurgen was going to do a performance. Braun primed a loaf of bread with rubber cement, set light to it and placed it on his head. The result was spectacular but safe – flames leapt from the highly inflammable rubber cement, while the bread safely insulated Jurgen's head from any danger. While his bread hat burnt, Braun chanted a list of names and did a little dance.

Two police officers arrived. There'd been a report of a black magic ritual taking place in the street. When Mark explained that the Flaming Chapatti Opening was an art event, they smiled indulgently and left.

Once those who were going home had departed, James snuggled up to Judy and Hazel stumbled drunkenly into Mark's room – where she fell into his data installation, demolishing it. Mark spent most of the night dismantling the remains and putting them in order – while Hazel lay curled up in his bed and Peter Murray tried to catch some sleep on the floor. In the room above Mark's, John was in bed with Gloria Swann, Person Person with Birgit Smith and Brett Johnson with Adrian Foster.

JAMES GOT UP AT NINE-THIRTY, Judy ten minutes later. Person Person was rousing his room-mates from their sleep. Mark, Hazel and Peter had left the house and were eating breakfast in a cafe on Kennington Road.

People wondered in and out of the kitchen. At 11.15am, James, Judy, Mark, Peter, Person, Gloria, Jurgen and Marianne left the house and caught a 159 bus from Kennington Park to Trafalgar Square, they then walked the minimal distance to Canada House where the Neoist Video Screening was scheduled to start at noon. Stephen Brady arrived just before twelve and a couple of others just after. The videos were tedious. A few members of the general public wandered innocently in and then very quickly walked out. The screenings dragged on until 5.30pm, a marathon endurance test. James decided to give the evening's activities, 'live action and exchanges', a miss – instead he headed home.

THE NEOISTS WERE SCHEDULED TO MEET at noon on Lambeth Bridge – to shoot a scene for Jurgen's film In Search Of The Great Mr Pighead. In this episode, a group of English artists would try to prevent Jurgen crossing the Thames. Jurgen, Mark, Judy, Peter, Marianne, Person, Birgit and Gloria arrived twenty minutes late. James and Charles White were waiting for them. Brett Johnson, Stephen Brady and Rupert Swiftwood – a rich friend of Mark's – were almost an hour late.

Jurgen put on one of his many Neoist hats – in this instance a large fish that had been slit open and gutted. Thus attired, he was ready for rehearsals. It was 2pm before the filming was completed.

JAMES AND JUDY ARRIVED AT the London Musicians Collective at six-thirty. Mark and Peter had already set up the necessary equipment for the opening act of The Popular Chapatti Circus. Seeing that everything was in hand – and not wishing to do anything themselves – James and Judy retired to the pub across the road. As the evening wore on, they were joined by Terry Wood and Fiona Roberts – a friend of Terry's from his home town of Lymm – Jurgen, Marianne, Stephen Brady, Person, Birgit, Gloria and Rupert Swiftwood

Just after eight, Mark dragged everyone out of the pub and into the Musicians Collective. The event had been advertised as being open to the public – but no paying customers arrived. An evening of performances, music, slides, video, installations, readings, films and free hair cuts was apparently not to the public's taste.

JAMES AND JUDY GOT UP AT ELEVEN-THIRTY. Mark and Jurgen were setting up video equipment in preparation for the Chapatti Armchair Revolution, which was scheduled to run from noon until six. The event was to take place around a table placed in the street, so that anyone who happened to be passing could participate.

Gloria Swann, who had left number thirteen very early that morning, arrived home with her entourage – which consisted of Stephen Brady and a young film-maker called Alan Philips. It was one-forty before the Armchair Revolution actually commenced. Alan Philips left after about an hour. A break in the filming of this event coincided with the arrival of Thomas, the junkie from number eleven, who upset everybody by shooting up in front of them.

The afternoon wore on, with only endless cups of tea to help it wear off. Thomas gazed up at the sun and mumbled something about UFOs.

Conversations sputtered along – with every incoherent syllable being filmed. Mark shaved Person's head, leaving two tufts of hair at the back, which he shaped into an inverted question mark. Using a marker pen, he then drew a brain on Person's scalp.

A passer-by stopped and pointed at Person.

'Gawd, what's the matter with 'im?' she exclaimed and then proceeded on her way.

The old woman's interjection was the only eventful moment of the afternoon. The Armchair Revolution ended early and Mark, with a little help from Peter, packed up the video equipment and loaded it into the hire van they'd parked on Milverton Street. Gloria and Stephen left to attend a Jennifer Binnie private view.

At six forty-five there was a mass exit from number thirteen. Hazel joined the crew as they walked from the Place to Milverton Street. She'd almost missed her lift to the Musicians Collective.

The evening was not particularly eventful. Again there were no paying customers. To James' surprise, he didn't find his performance with Judy in the least bit embarrassing.

AT ELEVEN-THIRTY THE NEXT MORNING, Mark filmed the introduction to The Neoist Guide Dog. Person had donned a dog mask and was crawling about on all fours. Birgit was wearing a pair of dark glasses and carrying a white stick, so that she could play the part of a blind woman. Birgit was led to the Elephant and Castle by her 'dog.' From here, she caught a bus to Greenwich Park, where the Neoist Time Picnic was scheduled to take place. Unfortunately, heavy rain resulted in this event being canceled.

In the evening, Judy made a sound sculpture. She gathered everyone in the kitchen at Aulton Place, handed round packets of crisps and recorded them being eaten. At ten, Jurgen ushered the assembled troops into the back garden, where – under the light of the stars – he performed a burial ceremony for the fish he'd worn as a hat on Lambeth Bridge.

THE NEOIST ARMADA FROM LAMBETH PIER commenced half-an-hour later than scheduled. It was a rainy Saturday afternoon. The Neoists had made toy boats to launch on the Thames. Mark persuaded Person to film him setting fire to a glue-soaked pair of overalls which he'd somehow succeeded in getting to float – and then documented the other Neoists launching their creations.

In the evening, the Chapatti Extinguishing Ceremony consisted of Mark taking a portrait photograph of each Neoist and then recording taped interviews with his subjects – thus creating a 'solid audio document' for posterity.

JAMES AND JUDY GOT UP AT NOON. They'd been woken by the sound of Mark and Hazel rowing. They were still dressing when Hazel stormed out of the house. When they went to get their breakfast, Mark left the kitchen without returning their greetings. James ate the bacon and eggs Judy put in front of him, then told her he was going home.

James walked to the phone box on Kennington Road, rifled through his pockets – he had Hazel's number somewhere and she'd had enough time to get home.

'Hello.'

'Hello, Hazel, it's James, are you alright?'

'Yeah.'

'Listen, maybe I could come over and see you.'

'Yeah, that would be nice.'

'We could go for a walk and maybe get a drink later on.'

'I'll see you later.'

'Okay.'

'Bye for now then.'

'Bye.'

When James got to East Dulwich, Hazel seemed really pleased to see him.

'So what happened between you and Mark?'

'I made a remark about Jurgen and it led to an argument over the status of modern art. Mark got really mad when I told him that what he did was a waste of time.'

James and Hazel walked down to Dulwich Park. They left the park just after six and stopped in a pub on their way home. Hazel bought two bottles of Pils and they sat in the beer garden drinking them. When they'd finished the round, James went and bought more lager. When it got dark, they moved into the pub. James put his arm around Hazel.

'I really fancy you,' he whispered and then kissed her. 'You're the best looking girl in the world.'

Hazel slipped his arm off her shoulder.

'Don't, it's wrong, I'm too old for you. You should be seeing girls like those over there,' she pointed at two teenagers, 'not old women like Judy and me.'

'You're not old, you're beautiful,' James whispered.

He slipped his arm around her and kissed her again. This time, Hazel made no attempt to stop him. They walked home with their arms wrapped around each other. James was not quite as drunk as he was pretending to be. Hazel got some wine from the kitchen.

'What are we going to do with you? We can't put you in Dave's room, he'll be back later on.'

James put his arms around Hazel.

'I'll sleep with you.'

'We're going to regret this,' she whispered.

Part 4

A New Dawn

Assessing the Art Strike

THERE ARE MANY WAYS IN WHICH it's possible to deal with the Art Strike. For instance, it's been explained as a conceptual art piece consisting of all the propaganda calling on cultural workers to stop making or discussing their work from January 1st 1990 to January 1st 1993 – along with the various responses with which this demand has been met. It will become clear during the course of this talk that I don't concur with this view because in my opinion, the Art Strike would not have generated so much publicity or confusion if it had been produced as an art work.

Early in 1989, a year before the Art Strike began, I wrote that 'the time for theorising the Art Strike will be after it has taken place.' This statement was one of a number grouped under the heading *No Theoretical Summing Up*. Like the Art Strike, at first glance these words appear to be little more than a flat refusal to engage in a discourse that might be of value to the culture industry. However, both this statement – and the Art Strike in general – work on more than one level. In the case of the fourteen words I've chosen to cite, taken in context, they also point towards a rather unoriginal view of history as something created after the fact by academics sitting amongst dusty piles of books – rather than by the Napoleons and Bismarcks who are familiar to us from dimly remembered school lessons. I'm digressing, and that's highly appropriate considering that I've stated on more than one occasion that the Art Strike was located in opposition to closure.

You've probably gathered by now that I'm unwilling to nail the Art Strike down. I've no wish to provide some monolithic theoretical justification for the Art Strike now that it's taken place. There's no simple explanation of what the Art Strike was about because it was simultaneously a hammer blow delivered to the heart of the cultural establishment and a very clever career move. After looking through the boxes of Art Strike material that have been gathering dust in my flat, I know that it's impossible to do justice to the omnidirectional nature of the Art Strike in the time it will take to deliver this lecture.

In an attempt to trace the genesis of the Art Strike, I'm going to backtrack to 1982. I was twenty years old and wanted to put life back into the corpse of the revolutionary avant garde. I was determined to create a Frankenstein's monster that would destroy the humourless cliques I used to run into who talked about Surrealism as 'unfinished business' and the Situationist International as having produced 'the ultimate anti-capitalist critique'.

Fortunately, I'd already hit upon plagiarism as a technique with which to antagonise my adversaries. I didn't need any ideas of my own, all I had to do was plunder the past. The first thing I came up with had a pedigree that goes back at least as far as the Berlin Dadaists – who'd declared that anyone who paid them fifty marks could be Jesus Christ. A more recent twist on the same theme is found in Julian Temple's film *The Great Rock'n'Roll Swindle*, which features a scene that sets out to prove that 'anybody can be a Sex Pistol'. I decided to enter the fray by issuing a series of leaflets which simultaneously demanded that all rock bands call themselves White Colours and that plagiarism should be adopted as a creative technique.

Two years later, I ran into various members of the Neoist Network and discovered that back in 1977, David Zack had issued a call for interested parties to assume the identity of an 'open pop star' named Monty Cantsin. Zack figured that if enough people used the name, this fictitious character would quickly develop a huge following and anybody who wanted a ready-made audience for their music would be able find one simply by billing themselves as Monty Cantsin. Since I'd been working along similar lines, I decided to throw in my lot with the Neoists. The younger members of the group were very receptive to 'my' ideas about plagiarism. Older Neoists such as Pete Horobin and tENTATIVELY a cONVENIENCE were more interested in inventing some new universal language. However, only R. U. Sevol and Istvan Kantor were openly hostile. Kantor soon changed his tune but the first time I met him, he ranted and raved about a statement I'd made claiming Lautreamont as a plagiarist when he considered it self-evident that the author of *Maldoror* was 'an original'.

Neoism was rooted in Fluxus, Mail Art and Punk. I was able to transform the movement by grafting on a direct link to the Situationist tradition. Much of this simply consisted of providing a 'radical' theoretical underpinning to the group's post-Fluxus activities (by blatantly plagiarising situationist texts) – alongside a vigorous use of plagiarism and the Monty Cantsin identity. Teenagers coming into the movement, such as John Berndt and Graf Haufen, took up these ideas and as a result, Neoism entered the final of it's four phases. Critics have often treated this final period as if it was characteristic of the entire history of Neoism – in fact, there are vast differences between the early period in Portland when Zack and Al Ackerman invented the movement, the activist phase of the Montreal group in 1979/80, the movement that then spread across the Western World and it's final transformation in my hands in 1984.

By April 1985 I was feeling frustrated. Neoism was a dead end. As a vehicle for 'my' ideas, this particular movement had taken them as far as they'd go in Neo-Dadaist clothing. This led me to make two important decisions – to end my involvement with Neoism and to plagiarise Gustav Metzger's 1974 proposal for an Art Strike. These two decisions were closely related. The Neoist movement had acquired so much historical baggage during the course of its development that the issues raised by the Art Strike would have been ignored by virtually everyone outside the group if this moratorium on the production of culture had been proclaimed under the aegis of Neoism. Although it was the last thing Dave Zack, Al Ackerman and Maris Kundzin intended when they founded the group, Neoism had become a self-consciously avant-garde movement and its intolerant attitude towards less rigorous sections of the cultural underground resulted in many individuals rejecting Neoist activities without actually giving them any serious consideration. Meanwhile, the Art Strike tied in very neatly with the interest I'd retained in plagiarism and collective pseudonyms – providing me with an opportunity to develop all three concepts. In fact, they quickly became so intertwined that it's become very difficult to talk about any one of them without referring to the other two – hence the need that will be encountered at various points in this talk for digressions on these intimately related subjects.

It's been suggested by a number of people that the Art Strike was simply a career move and/or a publicity stunt on my part. To treat the Art Strike like this is ludicrous because as a cultural phenomena it was anything but stable and static. In fact, the Art Strike went through several periods of uneven but dynamic development. One of the initial attractions the Art Strike held for me was that it placed a strict time limit on my post-Neoist activities. By propagating the interlinked concepts of plagiarism, multiple names and Art Strike (as a means of questioning Western notions of individuality, value and truth) I was able to resurrect the corpse of the revolutionary avant-garde – and then kill it off again after four and a half years.

The earliest propaganda I produced to promote the 1990 Art Strike was a straight plagiarism of Gustav Metzger's 1974 proposal with the dates changed from 1977-80 to 1990-93. However, since the 1977 Art Strike had been a complete flop, it was clear to me that I'd have to be more energetic than Metzger in promoting the concept. I began talking about the Art Strike as a 'refusal of creativity' and an act of class war carried on within the cultural sphere, as well as linking it to my use of plagiarism and multiple names. One of the major outlets for this propaganda was *Smile*, a magazine I'd founded in February 1984. Prior to making contact with the Neoists, I'd already been demanding that all magazines be called *Smile*. The early issues were produced with a typewriter. After my break with Neoism, the magazine became much smarter looking, with a glossy two colour cover and the text properly typeset.

At first I made little headway with the Art Strike, only John Berndt and Tony Lowes seemed interested in the idea. Perhaps the difficulties I encountered were partly due to the fact that despite the break I'd made, many people still associated my activities with Neoism. More important still, was the collage structure of *Smile*, which tended to overshadow it's content. Thus the number of individuals producing periodicals with that title multiplied because the cold, aggressive and apparently logical structure of my journal was undoubtedly impressive – but dazzled by the magazine's sense of style, the majority of readers either failed to take in or misunderstood what I was saying. I should perhaps at this point admit that this state of affairs was largely planned and had, in fact, become an integral part of my activities. As the style magazine *Blitz* commented in October 1986 'literary penetrability has never been high up *Smile*'s list of priorities'.

The mere existence of *Smile* enabled me to develop the multiple name concept but had the simultaneous effect of overshadowing my plagiarism and Art Strike projects. To rectify this situation, I set about organising a *Festival of Plagiarism* in London. Rather than simply participate in the event I'd organised, various individuals in the States decided to set up festivals of their own. Thus, in January 1988, there were simultaneous *Festivals of Plagiarism* in London, San Francisco and Madison, Wisconsin.

These were followed up with further events in Braunschweig (West Germany) and Glasgow (Scotland). As a result, the underground of Europe and the United States was flooded with plagiarist propaganda.

The various *Festivals of Plagiarism* were radically different from any of the Neoist Apartment Festivals and established to the satisfaction of most of those active in the cultural underground that I'd made a complete break with Neoism. More importantly, the organisers of the San Francisco *Festival of Plagiarism* were so pleased with the success of their event, that they decided to focus on the Art Strike as their next major project. Thus they organised an *Art Strike Mobilization Week* at the ATA Gallery in January 1989 and formed the first Art Strike Action Committee. Further Action Committees were quickly set up in London, Eire and Baltimore (USA).

During the summer of 1989, the underground was awash with Art Strike propaganda. By the end of the year, the Art Strike was receiving some mainstream media coverage – in the press, on tv and radio. I'd succeeded in making a reasonably large number of people reflect on the political implications of cultural production and infuriated a good many reactionaries who believed that rather than being a dull sham, art gave expression to so called spiritual values. In the process of doing this, I'd also made a name for myself, and going 'on strike' at the beginning of 1990 represented a far greater sacrifice than when I'd first announced this moratorium on cultural production.

It was this change in my circumstances that transformed what had initially been a ludic proposal into something more akin to a career move. Although very few of the fifty or so individuals who'd been most active in propagating the Art Strike took the proposal very seriously, I was determined to see the project through to its conclusion – and actually struck! As a result, I now appear to be the major force behind the Art Strike. Obviously, this obscures the fact that it took the collaboration of numerous other individuals to generate the interest and debate around the 1990 Art Strike that has not only validated a number of my own activities but also rescued Gustav Metzger's 1974 proposal from the complete oblivion which might otherwise have been its fate.

Given the number of scabs who ignored the 1990–93 moratorium on cultural production, it's perhaps extraordinary that I can report the Art Strike in the same triumphal fashion as the Situationist International wrote about the events of May 68. After the boom years of the late eighties, many galleries shut down long before the deep surgery of the years without art had resulted in the plug being pulled on the patient's life-support system. In an article entitled 'The Sinking of Cork Street', the *Guardian* reported on 29 May 1992 that: 'In the past two years one in four of the major galleries in the West End have closed due to... a shrinking market', and that there had been 'a reported 60 per cent drop in art sales'. The news that the art world was collapsing shouldn't have escaped any regular reader of the press, some other morale-boosting headlines included 'Dealers feel pinch as slump hits Art World' (*Guardian* 5/7/91) and 'You are invited to an Art World wake' (*Independent* (10/10/92) – while the 1993 New Year issue of *Time Out* reported the following gallery closures in its review of the previous twelve months: Anne Berthoud, Albemarle, Nicola Jacobs, Fabian Carlsson, Odette Gilbert, Maureen Paley, Milch and Nigel Greenwood. Obviously, the recession played a role in creating this pleasant state of affairs – but that needn't prevent me from claiming that the psychological impact of the Art Strike was largely responsible for this cultural crisis. Art Strike propaganda made it clear that simply challenging the implicit assumptions of serious culture would go a long way towards destroying its hegemony.

The three year period of the Art Strike also saw the world of serious fiction decimated, with a *Times* headline of 6 February 1992 announcing the 'Burial Rites of the Hardback'. Likewise, in his *Independent On Sunday* books review of the year 1992, Blake Morrison bemoaned the fact that unlike a decade ago, it was no longer possible to make a list of the best twenty young British novelists – he could only think of four and failed to add that the bozos he picked will soon have been forgotten. Other good news from the publishing industry included the suicide of literary hack Richard Burns, who hanged himself on 31 August 1992. Ian Katz in an article entitled 'Chronicle of a death foretold' (*Guardian* 14/12/92) quotes Robert Winder, literary editor of the *Independent*, as saying 'He had a new book about to come out. I wonder whether he sat down and read it and suddenly thought... I'm not Saul Bellow'. One assumes such a realisation would be a cause for celebration – and so it seems likely that Burns topped himself because the Art Strike shattered the hegemony of his elitist world view. The factor Winder highlights simply isn't credible – at least not to anyone whose not a member of that mythical society, the literary mafia.

It hardly needs stating that 1992 was by far and away the best year of the

Art Strike, as the obituary columns of the international press listed the deaths of numerous proponents of serious culture – including, Francis Bacon, John Cage, George MacBeth and John Piper. Although not quite so directly related to my Art Strike campaign, I was equally pleased to hear that Friedrich von Hayek and David Widgery had snuffed it. Of course, it's impossible to measure the impact of Art Strike propaganda on those who are now dead – but hopefully it hammered a few nails into the coffins of these hacks.

However, the Art Strike was more than simply an attack on high culture and at the beginning of the three year moratorium on cultural production, I not only ceased writing, producing graphics, organising events and playing the guitar – I also stopped promoting the Art Strike. As it turned out, there were other individuals – such as Lloyd Dunn in Iowa – who were very active in keeping the Art Strike alive as an issue of debate within the underground. Likewise, old Art Strike materials were still in circulation and thousands of people were exposed to them for the first time long after they'd passed out of my hands. In itself, this illustrates the long delays involved in the distribution of cultural products and ideas – and since I'd decided to allow all the materials I'd created prior to January 1st 1990 to circulate during the Art Strike, I'm now able to provide still further models of this process.

For example, on 12 December 1989, I finished work on a novel entitled *Defiant Pose*. However, the book wasn't published until June 1991, eighteen months after it was completed and nearly a year and three quarters since I'd first started work on it. The fact that *Defiant Pose* made the books of the year lists in *The Face* and *Gay Times* of December 1991, and the best of the worst in the *Sunday Times* review of the literary year, amply reflects the fact that none of the works chosen were written during the twelve months in question. Therefore, the Art Strike can be read as my way of giving critics a chance to catch up with what I'd been doing during the eighties. And not only critics! The Art Strike also gave cultural administrators the opportunity to get to grips with my work. The last time I gave a public lecture was in December 1989, like this talk that one was also on the Art Strike – but my speech of three years ago was given at the Institute of Contemporary Arts, whereas today I've been booked into the more prestigious Victoria and Albert Museum. Individual reputations very rarely stand still in the cultural world and the Art Strike proves that doing nothing is often more productive than desperately seeking fame and fortune.

At this point, I'd like to backtrack to my books. My first novel, *Pure Mania*, was originally scheduled for publication in May 1989 – but due to various disputes between the imprint I was dealing with and their parent company, it didn't actually see the light of day until December 1989. Although I did some publicity for the book, once I hit my January 1st deadline, I refused to do any more interviews. The offers I turned down included the opportunity to appear on the *Jonathan Ross Show* – which should be an indication of how seriously I took the Art Strike. Accepting these invitations would have done a lot more for my career than being one of two participants in a three year Art Strike. After the journal *Square Peg* ran a competition in which readers had to submit fake interviews with me, I thought I should respond to this challenge – and so when my second novel was published in June 1991, I sent other people along to do interviews for me. This didn't work out very well, since all the journalists concerned realised they were being duped – and in the end, I returned to flatly refusing to do interviews or personal appearances.

There was a ludic quality to turning down publicity opportunities and remunerative offers of work – the disbelief with which my refusals were met more than compensated me for the fact that I was passing up the possibility of fame and fortune. For a time, it even seemed likely that I'd become famous without actually producing any further work of my own – because a number of individuals were issuing texts supposedly written by Stewart Home, in an attempt to discredit the Art Strike. The industrial rock band Academy 23 did this most successfully by producing a magazine entitled *Smile*, allegedly in collaboration with me. Unfortunately, they cocked up by admitting in a 1992 interview that they hadn't seen me since 1985 and had no idea where I was living. Other individuals – such as Mark Bloch with his *Last Word* pamphlet – tried and failed to bait me into print by publishing blatant lies about certain of my activities during the eighties.

As I've already said, I'm not interested in theorising the Art Strike. I'll leave it to my critics to sort out the mess I created with the help of some friends. And there's an awful lot that requires elucidation – from the various ways in which I plundered the past, through to the influence of my activities on the KLF rock band and Michael Bogdanov founder of the English Shakespeare Company, who the *Independent On Sunday* of 3 January 1993 reported as calling for a 20 year moratorium on the production of plays by the bard. As Sadie Plant wrote in her book *The Most Radical Gesture* (Routledge, London and New York 1992): 'Carrying a provocative ambiguity which incited confusion, the Art Strike reintroduced a whole range of issues centred around questions of strategy, recuperation, and the relation between culture and politics'.

The quote from Plant's book should help clarify a statement I made at the beginning of 1989, to the effect that the Art Strike 'should be understood in terms of social psychology, as intuitive mental pictures, rather than actions which have been rationally theorised'. Somewhat like Sorel's conception of the General Strike, the Art Strike should be viewed as a myth that drove (wo)men to (in)action. The Art Strike was an organised myth that took hold of individual artists and encircled them, sapping the will and creating a sensation of helplessness. As was observed in some Art Strike propaganda, most artists appear to be nervous about what they do and feel anxious as to whether they perform a socially useful function. What the Art Strike made clear, is that artistic activities have no social value whatsoever and in fact are extremely wasteful. The recent collapse of Cork Street indicates that the number of individuals immobilised by the Art Strike was even greater than those who felt severely threatened by it and reacted with violent denunciation. We can therefore conclude that as propaganda and myth, the Art Strike was a great success.

Notes for lecture at Victoria and Albert Museum
30 January 1993

Our tactics against Stockhausen

KARLHEINZ STOCKHAUSEN COMPOSES modern classical music that is highly regarded by consumers of 'serious culture' and very rarely performed. Recently, the clarinettist Ian Stuart has been touring Britain with a show that includes a rendition of Stockhausen's *Harlequin*. Despite the status accorded to Stockhausen and Stuart as representatives of 'high art', their activities are completely vacuous. Ken Rea, writing in the *Guardian* on 21/5/93, had the following to say about *Harlequin*: 'This extraordinary solo requires him (Ian Stuart) to dance while playing the clarinet... Written in 1975 as a showcase for Stockhausen's partner Suzanne Stephens, the composition was so taxing that she collapsed after the first performance... It is notable enough to see a classical musician play a 45-minute solo from memory, but dancing in lycra tights at the same time is another matter.' What impresses 'critics' of 'serious culture' is the technique required to perform the piece. Rea leaves his readers with the impression that because giving a rendition of *Harlequin* is physically challenging, this validates the composition as a work of art. Clearly such a supposition is nonsense, *Harlequin* functions as 'serious culture' because Stockhausen and Stuart have successfully negotiated their way through a complex set of social and institutional practices. Put another way, *Harlequin* is 'high art' because those in positions of cultural power say it is a 'great' composition, while simultaneously treating other forms of music – for example Oi! – as worthless trash.

To draw attention to this state of affairs, the Neoist Alliance decided to disrupt Ian Stuart's performance of Harlequin at the Pavilion Theatre, Brighton, on 15 May 1993. This was not the first time Stockhausen had been targeted as a particularly obnoxious representative of 'high art'. Armed with placards bearing the slogan 'FIGHT RACIST MUSIC', Action Against Cultural Imperialism picketed his concert at the Judson Hall, New

York, on 8 September 1964. Likewise, during the early seventies, Cornelius Cardew instigated a vociferous critique of idealism in culture that culminated with the publication of *Stockhausen Serves Imperialism* (Latimer, London 1974). Although the Neoist Alliance does not agree with all the points raised in these previous critiques of Stockhausen and his music, we felt the Ian Stuart concert provided an excellent opportunity to take militant action against the cultural faction of the ruling class.

The first thing we did was produce a leaflet asking the public to 'BOYCOTT STOCKHAUSEN'. A press release was also circulated in which it was stated that the Neoist Alliance would levitate the Pavilion Theatre during the concert. As a result, a story appeared in the *Brighton and Hove Leader* on 13/5/93 entitled 'Composer Is Set To Reach New Heights'. There was also coverage on Festival Radio, including a brief interview with a Neoist Alliance spokesperson. Stockhausen has claimed that much of his music is dictated to him by beings from a superior civilisation who live in a distant galaxy. The propaganda of the Neoist Alliance was designed to expose the mystical aura in which the composer shrouds his works as a blatant fraud.

As the Neoist Alliance and its supporters gathered outside the Pavilion Theatre prior to the Stockhausen concert, they were met by a counter-demonstration organised by the Temple Ov Psychic Youth. The TOPY activists were worried that if we successfully levitated the Pavilion Theatre, 'a negative vortex would be created which could seriously damage the ozone layer'. Neoist Alliance members were dressed in dark suits and ties, which contrasted sharply with the scruffy casual wear of the counter-demonstrators. We'd also brought placards. On one side of these there was a cartoon of a bomb and the words 'DEMOLISH SERIOUS CULTURE', on the other, a pyramid capped by the all seeing eye and the message 'WE'RE BACK'.

As the handful of individuals who'd decided to cross the picket line arrived for the concert, they were met with chants of 'Boycott Stockhausen' from our ranks, to which the TOPY activists replied with cries of 'Stop The Levitation'. The counter-demonstrators pleaded with concert-goers to remain outside the building so that they could participate in a set of breathing and visualisation exercises designed to prevent the levitation. Once the concert began, the two sets of demonstrators prepared themselves for a psychic battle outside the theatre. These street actions drew a far larger crowd than the Ian Stuart recital inside the building. Passers-by were reluctant to step in front of the waves of psychic energy we were generating and soon much of the street was at a standstill. The *Brighton and Hove Leader* of 20/5/93 quoted one shaken concert-goer as saying, 'I definitely felt my chair move. It shook for a minute and then stopped.' The Neoist Alliance also received reports of toilets overflowing and electrical equipment short-circuiting, although these went unreported by the press.

While TOPY were adamant that their actions prevented the Pavilion Theatre being raised 25 feet into the air, the Neoist Alliance considers the protest to have been a complete success. The campaign against Stockhausen is part of an on-going struggle that will continue until the last apologist for decadent 'high art' has been silenced! Actions like the one we undertook in Brighton chip away at the confidence of the arts establishment and expose 'serious culture' as a monstrous fraud perpetrated by a self-serving elite.

First published in *Variant* 15
Autumn 1993

The burial rites of literary fiction

LAST TIME I SAW THE WRITER MICHAEL BRACEWELL, he was depressed because his work had been 'overlooked' by the bozos judging the 20 Best Young British Novelists award. This scam had been cooked up by the abysmal *Granta Magazine* as a way of recouping some of the losses it had incurred in its ludicrous attempts to project itself as being at the cutting edge of culture. Not only did publishers have to pay to have their authors entered into the competition, if their 'protégés' won, they had to fork out even more dosh to cover the costs of the promotion. Personally, I'm proud that I've never been nominated for a literary award because its patently obvious that young writers whose work meets with immediate acceptance by the publishing industry are doing no more than reproducing the bankrupt formulas of preceding generations.

While I'm ambitious enough to want to reinvent world culture in its entirety, most of the authors I meet aspire to nothing more than being as famous as Martin Amis or some other untalented hack. Unlike the majority of young English writers, I consider the opinions of the literary establishment worthless and am not prepared to pander to their tastes in a bid to win acceptance and fame. Besides, fame should be a by-product of achievement, the fact that so many people today covet it as a thing in itself shows only that degraded minds are incapable of understanding philosophical egoism. Schopenhauer observed in *The Wisdom Of Life* that: 'The general history of art and literature shows that the highest achievements of the human mind are, as a rule, not favourably received at first; but remain in obscurity until they win notice from intelligence of a higher order, by whose influence they are brought into a position which they maintain, in virtue of the authority thus given them.'

Recently, English 'literature' has found its perfect representative in Will Self, whose collection of short stories *The Quantity Theory Of Insanity* won the Geoffrey Faber Memorial Prize and who was selected as one of the 20 Best Young British Novelists before he'd published a novel. Self told the ultra-conservative *ES Magazine* in September '93 that it is an advantage to be 'white, middle-class, male and Oxbridge', however, he has also read Burroughs and so his establishment publisher promotes him as a rebel and an outsider. 'I don't belong in the mainstream,' Self snivels, 'and 25 years ago it would have been impossible.' What Self fails to explain is that it would have been impossible to imitate Martin Amis, although this wouldn't have presented him with a problem because he'd simply have copied some other hack. The quaintness of Self's views is readily evident in the fact that despite years of po-mo theorising, he doesn't consider the notion of 'mainstream' to be even slightly problematic.

In conversation with the critic Elizabeth Young, Self has made even sillier claims. Not only does he believe that there is no longer an underground, he also thinks that mainstream publishers will print anything. This is exactly what the corporate publishers want to hear, suddenly they can pretend to be the cutting edge! However, as I've observed elsewhere, the book trade exists to prevent energetic, exciting and innovative work being published. The publishing industry is not consciously organised as a conspiracy against youth and vigour but acts as such because good 'taste' dictates that 'writers' replicate the ideals of a long gone and unlamented age. Self told *ES Magazine* that he might become a 'situationist', thereby demonstrating that he'd failed to attain even the most elementary grasp of the movement of (post) modern culture.

The avant-garde is fluid and while a critique of the institution of art is central to it, both the dominant culture and those passing historical judgement upon contemporary 'literature', transform themselves and each other over time. The situationists are now a historical group and while it is necessary to gather up and internalise the past, in doing so we should transform it. Marx stated in *The Eighteenth Brumaire*, and it has since become a cliché, that: 'Men make their own history, but not of their own free will, not under circumstances they themselves have chosen but under the given and inherited circumstances with which they are directly confronted'. Likewise, Raoul Vaneigem noted in *The Revolution Of Everyday Life*, that what's required to free our creative abilities from the fetters imposed upon them by the gangsters who run this world, is the conjunction of nihilism and historical consciousness.

It is now a banality to repeat Bakunin's maxim that 'the urge to destroy is also a creative urge'. However, this saying serves to illustrate the dual nature of the movement 'progress' requires from 'authors' whose 'writing' is so fresh that they don't know how to spell – and don't need to know, because the software that came with their PCs included a dictionary and a thesaurus. Culture is running amok, with genre cross-fertilising genre and endless graphic sex. The rising generation doesn't give a shit about characterisation, measured prose or literary merit. Slapstick, brutality and violence are the weapons being marshalled against decorum and good taste. *ES Magazine* makes it quite clear whose interests Self represents: 'he is... a bulwark against the corrosive effects of interactive media. The development of CD-ROM has created 'living books' where text amalgamates with sound. These and other digital innovations could push paper publishing off the map – writing as a source of cultural authority could become less revered.' And, of course, this would be a benefit to everyone who hasn't got their nose stuck into the literary gravy train.

In himself, Self, the literary serf, is inconsequential. However, like the Rugby school educated child of privilege Salman Rushdie, who hails his young comrade as 'a cult figure', Self represents vested interest, literary feudalism and the triumph of cultural mediocrity. Establishment publishers have long been unwilling to sign up talented writers because when books of merit are given decent distribution, they blow the self-indulgent garbage that passes itself off as literature right out of the water. In any case, those who represent the wave of the future are not interested in publication between hard covers, they see such frivolities as the myopic vice of imbeciles hooked on self-abuse. Instead, intelligence is storming the infobahn and exposing the totalitarian nature of a dominant culture that considers criticism of Rushdie taboo.

The fiction that hacking together a novel requires talent is an untenable myth. The literary establishment is a joke, dead on its feet and not worth mourning. The effete garbage it passes off as art is being trampled underfoot. The past is a useless cipher, a code for a programme that no longer exists. Now that word processing has supplanted writing, no one wants to read works that were originally drafted in pen and ink. What I aim for in my activities is an ambiguity on a par with that achieved by Machiavelli, who has been read as both a supporter of monarchical despotism and a republican using a rhetorical device to expose the mechanisms of political domination. Unfortunately, in England, it is still necessary to do away with the anchored authorial voice and associated notions inherited from nineteenth-century literature, such as introspection and characterisation. Here, the traditions of the dead generations still weigh like a nightmare on the minds of the living. Let the dead bury their dead, we will blaze a trail to new modes of being.

Large parts of this have previously appeared under the title 'Return Of The Repressed' in the *American Book Review*. However, it also contains several previously unpublished sentences, while those parts of the ABR article pasted in from my lecture 'Strategies Of Writing' have been deleted.

Programme of the Neoist Alliance

1 Religious
To undermine all monotheistic creeds and to propagate crazy cults, mysticism, para-science and anti-philosophies.

2 Ethical
To introduce debasing codes and practices, corrupt morals, weaken the marriage-bond, destroy family life and abolish inheritance.

3 Aesthetic
To foster the cult of the ugly and whatever is debasing, decadent and degenerate in music, literature, and the visual arts.

4 Sociological
To break up large corporations and abolish privilege. To provoke envy, discontent, revolt and class war.

5 Industrial and Financial. To lower the ideals of craftsmanship and abolish pride in handicraft. To encourage standardisation and specialisation. To wrest control of finance from the corrupt ruling class.

6 Political
To secure control over the press, broadcasting, cinema, stage and all means of influencing public opinion. To break up ruling class institutions from inside by creating dissensions.

Our tactics against the literary establishment

"WHEN 'HIGH ART' HACK RICHARD BURNS hanged himself, the literary establishment responded by wringing its hands. Once year on, it's high time book bores like Salman Rushdie, Martin Amis and Julian Barnes wrung their own necks. To encourage these parasites to top themselves and simultaneously celebrate the Richard Burns suicide anniversary, the Neoist Alliance is organising a psychic attack on the book trade."

These were the opening lines of a leaflet the Neoist Alliance began distributing in June. As the *Times Literary Supplement* reported (30/7/93), the aim was to make it clear to the literati that hardback fiction has no social value whatsoever and is, in fact, a form of mental pollution. The coverage of our activities in the *TLS*, *Time Out* (25/8/93) and *New Statesman* (10/9/93) all omitted to mention that this action was intended to celebrate the first anniversary of the suicide of literary novelist Richard Burns. The Neoist Alliance had breached the cultural establishment's code of good taste and the result was a partial censorship in the reporting of our activities.

Having mailed copies of these leaflets to numerous authors, editors and agents, word soon filtered back to us that our 'beastly' activities had the literati choking on their wine as they discussed the Neoist threat at dinner parties. Despite the partial media black out on the suicide celebration, we'd made sure that everyone in the book world knew exactly what was going on. The fury we provoked proved a point that had been made in our leaflet, namely that most of those actively promoting literature feel anxious about their work and are uncertain as to whether it performs a socially useful function.

Having sent one set of shock waves rumbling through the literary establishment, the Neoist Alliance proceeded to compound the damage by distributing fake Booker Prize invitations to down and outs. The small orange cards carried the following message: 'FREE BOOZE, NOSH & STRIPPERS at 6pm on Tuesday 26 October at the Guildhall, Aldermanbury, London EC2. A NIGHT OUT FOR THE HOMELESS Organised by THE BOOKER BENEVOLENT FUND. This card admits one person only.'

By this time, the literati were up in arms over the activities of the Neoist Alliance and had imposed unofficial sanctions against our organisation. Although cards and a press release were distributed to literary critics, there was no way they were going to cover this story! It was left to the *Sun* (7/9/93), to break the news with a page three item headlined 'Prize Night Freebie Is A Strip-Off!'. Taking its lead from the tabloids, the *Guardian* ran the story the following day. We were successfully spreading our message beyond the tiny coterie of book bores who control English fiction. Better still, the scumbags we'd attacked were smarting because they're not used to being described as pompous gits who need to be brought down to earth!

Simultaneously, news broke that the workers sacked from a Booker mushroom farm in Yorkshire planned to organise a BAN THE BOOKER demonstration outside the Guildhall on the night of the prize ceremony. Believing it was pointless to have two separate demonstrations taking place on the night, the Neoist Alliance cancelled its own operation and instructed sympathisers to support the sacked workers instead. The *Evening Standard* (27/10/93), in a news story headlined *Free Booze and Strippers but still no Booker Demo*, claimed that 'the enemies of order, middle-class literature and socialites in dickie bows and posh frocks failed to mass a mob... to terrorise the assorted grandees and intellectuals gathering... for the biggest night in the literary calendar'.

Smears of this type reveal just how desperate book bores have become to discredit the Neoist Alliance. The *Standard* also quoted our press release as saying: 'we are against the book trade because it exists to prevent energetic, exciting and innovative work being published'. The fact that this quote was wrenched out of context has led us to consider revising the sentence that followed it. Perhaps we were wrong to suggest that: 'the publishing industry is not consciously organised as a conspiracy against youth and vigour but acts as such because good 'taste' dictates that 'writers' replicate the ideals of a long gone and unlamented age'.

First published in *Variant* 16 Winter/Spring 1994

Neoism as negation and the negation of Neoism

THERE ARE MANY WAYS IN WHICH it's possible to explain the phenomena of Neoism. A prosaic history of the movement would probably suggest that Neoism started life as No Ism, a concept invented during the late seventies by David Zack, Al Ackerman and Maris Kundzin in Portland, Oregon. No Ism was an open, inclusive and anti-ideological grouping of individuals who saw themselves as artists opposed to the gallery system. This idea was transmitted to a group of French Canadians via Istvan Kantor who'd fled Hungary on a student visa after David Zack enticed him to decamp to North America with the aid of some colour xeroxes. Kiki Bonbon and the rest of the crowd Kantor befriended in Montreal then hit upon the idea of transforming No Ism into Neoism and parodying the legacy of the twentieth-century avant-garde.

The French Canadians had a gang mentality and Kantor found himself on the fringes of the group. Bonbon and his pals called their Hungarian friend 'grandpa' because he was in his early thirties. In an attempt to overcome his isolation, Kantor cultivated international contacts. Individuals such as tENTATIVELY a cONVENIENCE in Baltimore and Peter Below in Germany got involved with the group but Kantor remained a fringe figure who never fully understood the Neoist project. Kantor's cluelessness as to what was going on around him is legendary. Al Ackerman once told me that when Kantor arrived in Portland in 1978, the Hungarian was informed a mentally retarded man who hung out with Zack would act as his manager and get his singing career off to a flying start. As the weeks passed, Kantor became increasingly abusive about the retard, regularly indulging in hysterical fits where he'd scream 'this guy is useless, he's supposed to be my manager but he hasn't got me any gigs'. Once he settled in Montreal, Kantor lived off the extremely generous Canadian grant system for the arts and established a reputation as a tame performance artist who was happy to work within the gallery system. In stark contrast to this, the bulk of the Neoist Network was made up of potential iconoclasts who spent much of their time challenging consensus reality. However, Kantor's conventionality resulted in much of the press coverage the Neoists received during their early days focusing on him as an individual. Such verbiage now looks ridiculous – but rather than proceeding with a conventional interpretation of Neoism, I'm going to be more elliptical in my approach to the subject.

Allegorically, Neoism could be explained in the following fashion – during the middle ages there were a succession of heresies that have been described by the historian Norman Cohn as mystical anarchism. Adherents to these creeds believed that all goods should be held in common and that many things considered sinful by the Roman Catholic Church were in fact virtues when practised by the elect. Ranked among the more interesting of these sects are the Bohemian Adamites. On 21 October 1421, four hundred trained soldiers moved against the Adamite heretics and virtually wiped them out. By a miracle, their leader – known both as 'Adam' and 'Moses' – escaped to Prague. 'Adam' then took on a disciple, who in his turn, trained up a further initiate after his master's death. In this way, the Adamite creed was passed down through the ages and the Neoist Network is simply a contemporary manifestation of this ancient heresy. Viewing Neoism through the prism of this allegory makes imagery associated with the group accessible to those who have not been initiated into its ranks. When the Neoists speak about Akademgorod as their 'promised land', this is actually a code name for Prague. According to Neoist eschatology, Prague is the omphalos of our planet and once the movement seizes control of the city, the ancient Adamite plan of world domination will be effortlessly realised.

In keeping with this allegorical interpretation of Neoism, the initiation of individuals into the movement must necessarily be described as follows: the candidate is blindfolded and led into a darkened room. The fourteen secret masters of the world (or at least a group of available Neoists) interrogate the initiate. As a sign of obedience to the order, the candidate must answer 'yes' to a series of ninety-five questions. After this humiliating set-piece – in which the initiate admits to being a complete sexual failure – the candidate is fucked by every member of the lodge and then symbolically reborn by the removal of the blindfold. If this sounds an unlikely allegory, it's only because the story is – to an extent – literally true. John Berndt was kept blindfolded for a period of seven days during the so called *'Millionth' Neoist Apartment Festival*. During this time he was subjected to gropings and other sexual stimulations, made to carry dangerously sharp objects on the New York subway in the rush hour, had his usual sleep patterns completely disrupted, was flipped upside down and forced to run on his hands, &c.

Unfortunately, no one ever succeeded in ordering the rather loosely organised Neoist Network into a masonic structure. Pete Horobin made a brave attempt with his Data Cell project but this operation was ultimately a failure. Of the various twentieth-century avant-garde movements, only the Surrealists and the Situationist International came anywhere close to replicating the classic structure of a secret society. Until 1984, Neoism was most obviously influenced by Futurism, Dada, Fluxus, Mail Art and Punk. I managed to forge a few links with the Situationist tradition after joining the group but my comrades lacked the discipline to make the most of this input. Ultimately, Neoism derives the little historical importance it can now claim from the fact that it acted as a false dawn prior to my organisation of the far more significant Plagiarist and Art Strike movements.

The Neoists wanted to avoid any single meaning being imposed on their activities and believed that by bombarding their movement with a series of contradictory interpretations, they would split the meme and simultaneously create a monadic earthquake fierce enough to destroy world culture in its entirety. Thus Neoism was viewed simultaneously as modernist, post-modernist, an avant-garde transgression of modern and post-modern traditions, as underground, Neo-Dadaist and an outgrowth of Fluxus. It was also a rejection of all these things.

Like every other avant-garde group, the Neoists hoped to project an image of themselves as the very latest trend in culture and this accounts for the more archaic aspects of their project. The occult elements provided a perfect counterpoint to the movement's faddish innovations, making these appear even more new-fangled and up-to-the-minute. It was a technique that had been employed very successfully by the Dadaists, Surrealists and Situationists.

Ultimately, the Neoist project was a failure because most of those involved with the group paid no heed to the lessons to be learnt from the critique of the image made by the Situationists and within Auto-Destructive Art. While the details of Situationist theory are fatally flawed – partially due to Debord's obsession with the Stuart succession – the notion of the spectacle is still of some use to those who wish to break with the world as it is and create a new tomorrow.

The avant-garde is in many ways a return of the repressed, the re-emergence of Protestant iconoclasm in a post-Christian world where art serves as a secular religion justifying the activities of a murderous ruling class. For example, in 1441 Hugh Knight went into a Cornish church and burnt the chin off a statue of the Virgin Mary. The result was a work in which the Virgin appeared to have grown a beard, making this act of image-breaking an important precursor to Duchamp's moustached Mona Lisa.

The Specto-Situationist obsession with text is an inevitable result of the group's assault on the image. Guy Debord would have felt very much at home if he'd ever had the opportunity to hang out with the Bible-thumping Lollards of the middle ages. The word is sacred, idolatry (the dominance of the Spectacle) an ever-lasting sin. Before heaven is realised on earth and every wo/man can live in their own cathedral, the word must be accepted and the sensuous image stamped into the ground by a legion of jack-booted Debordists. The critique of the image made by Gustav Metzger, who used acid to simultaneously create and destroy 'auto-destructive' works, was a far more incisive response to Judaic, Islamic and Protestant traditions of iconoclasm than that of the Specto-Situationists.

While I remained within the Neoist Network, I was unable to synthesise these and other forms of contemporary iconoclasm. After breaking with Neoism, I announced the 1990 Art Strike which brought together innumerable types of idol breaking. Once I'd fashioned this coffin for the corpse of art and defiantly nailed my ninety-five theses to the lid, the Neoists realised they'd been decisively outflanked. It was at this point that they began to claim my post-Neoist activities as an integral part of their project.

Today, when a Neoist or one of their friends writes about the group, I become the chief star of the movement. Neoism is no longer an attempt at negation via the destruction of the meme. For the past five years, various ex-members of the group have attempted to claim successful examples of iconoclasm – such as the Art Strike – as being somehow related to their personal activities. And so, while Neoism is of no significance whatsoever and this is its most interesting attribute, the search for truth increasingly resembles a quest for an unholy grail. Although I split the meme in 1985, what actually matters is how long news of this achievement takes to spread among the various populations of the world.

Written in April 1993 for the forthcoming Creation Press publication *Negation: The Last Book* edited by Jack Sergeant

Doctorin' our culture

DO YOU WANT TO 'DIVIDE & KREATE', 'Kick Out The Clocks' or discover 'K Time'? These are the concepts Bill Drummond and Jimmy Cauty are promoting as part of their latest project, the K Foundation. In certain quarters, the adverts concocted by this organisation have been met with disbelief. Countless journalists seem convinced that Drummond and Cauty are simply throwing away the money they've earned from their pop hits on an expensive and pointless campaign. However, to anyone familiar with the history of the KLF and the various utopian currents that fuel the counterculture, these ads make a great deal of sense.

To understand the K Foundation, it's necessary to acquire some historical knowledge. For those not in the know, Drummond and Cauty have been active in the music business for many years. The first fruit of their collaboration was the single *All You Need Is Love*, released in March 1987. Drummond and Cauty promoted this attack on the media's coverage of AIDS with a graffiti campaign in which the slogan *Shag Shag Shag* was daubed over advertising hoardings.

Having made a mark as avant-hip satirists, the JAMS or Justified Ancients of Mu Mu (as the duo dubbed themselves at the time), consolidated their cult following with the release of an album entitled *1987 – What The Fuck's Going On?* The platter received rave reviews in the music press, although the record was soon suppressed by lawyers acting for ABBA who objected to the heavy sampling of their hit single *Dancing Queen*. Drummond and Cauty milked the legal proceedings for press coverage, then released a new version of the LP with all samples removed and detailed instructions on how to recreate the original sound.

Further records followed under a bewildering variety of names, including Disco 2000 and the KLF. The duo had their first number one in 1988 with *Doctorin' The Tardis* which was credited to The Timelords. It was at this point that Drummond and Cauty began earning the money that currently finances the K Foundation. Stunt was followed by stunt and these pranks acted as adverts for a series of hit records. In April 1992, Drummond and Cauty dumped a dead sheep on the steps of the hotel where the Brit Awards ceremony was being held and then went on to be named Best British Group. The following month, the KLF placed a full page advert on the back of the NME announcing that they would not be releasing any new material in the foreseeable future and that their entire back catalogue was deleted.

A year later, the existence of the K Foundation was revealed in the first of a series of one page press advertisements. Having established an identity for the K Foundation, the campaign went into higher gear with the advice that 'TIME IS RUNNING IN… SWITCH TO K TIME NOW'. Then came an advert for a record that wasn't available. All three of these ads invited the public to send an SAE to a post office box for further information. To date, none of the people I know who wrote to this address have received a reply. Possibly the organisation has been swamped with requests for information because ads have appeared in the *NME*, *Guardian*, *Independent On Sunday* and *Sunday Times*.

The campaign took a new turn with the fourth ad in the series, which consisted of the slogan 'ABANDON ALL ART NOW' in letters nearly three inches high. After this came the announcement of the K Foundation Award, a forty thousand pound prize to be given to the artist who'd produced the worst body of work in the previous twelve months. The four nominees were identical to those chosen for the prestigious Turner Prize, which awards a mere twenty thousand pounds to its winner. The next ad in the campaign carried the headline 'LET THE PEOPLE CHOOSE' and a voting form, so that the public could have its say on who was the worst artist in the world.

From the beginning, what struck me about the campaign was the way in which it drew on the same underground and avant-garde sources that had inspired many of the KLF's finest moments. While Drummond and Cauty appear to be moving away from the pop industry, there is a deep sense of continuity between their earlier music based work and the recent advertising campaign.

One of the few influences on the KLF that music journalists have been able to pin down is that of Robert Anton Wilson and Robert Shea's Illuminatus novels. The historical material on which these books are based is part of a millenarial current that runs through western culture from the very beginning of the Christian era to the present day. These tendencies are given a more secular veneer in both communist and fascist doctrines. On the left, they are expressed in terms of 'the end of history'. The Nazi obsession with establishing 'a thousand year Reich' is a different formulation of very similar concerns. Likewise, the K Foundation's infatuation with time and its transformation is rooted in the same soil, although the branch to which Drummond and Cauty belong is that of mystical anarchism.

Springing from the same source, but to date not fully recognised as an influence on the KLF and K Foundation, is the twentieth-century tradition of avant-gardism. Movements such as the Futurists, Dadaists, Surrealists and Situationists are well known for the pranks they pulled on the cultural establishment. F. T. Marinetti paid for his *First Futurist Manifesto* to appear as an advertisement in *Le Figaro* of 20 February 1909. In this text, Marinetti spoke of his desire to 'destroy the museums, libraries and academies of every kind'. In other words, like the K Foundation campaign, Marinetti's Futurist advert was an attack on institutionalised art.

Drummond and Cauty have been described on numerous occasions as Situationists, but to label them as such is rather misleading. Situationism is simply one of many movements that make up the twentieth-century avant-garde tradition. The K Foundation are undoubtedly an outgrowth of this tradition but their work is not explicitly Situationist. Indeed, it has much more in common with the Neoist, Plagiarist and Art Strike movements of the nineteen-eighties than with the avant-garde of the fifties and sixties.

Obviously, the KLF (Kopyright Liberation Front) shared an interest in plagiarism with the eighties avant-garde. Over the past decade, columnists for avant-garde magazines such as *Photo Static* and *Vital* have spent a great deal of time ranting about why xerox machines and sampling technology make all existing copyright laws redundant. Likewise, during the eighties, a series of *Festivals of Plagiarism* were held in Europe and North America so that those concerned with these issues could meet and promote their cause. Drummond and Cauty drew on the heated discussion taking place everywhere from unofficial galleries to small circulation magazines and transformed it into something capable of setting the pop charts alight.

Another concern of the eighties avant-garde was with the use of multiple names as a means of raising questions about the nature of identity. By 1986, fifty different avant-garde magazine editors were calling their publications *Smile,* which of course caused a great deal of confusion. Even more people were using the name Karen Eliot – so that countless pictures, articles and songs, were produced by an artist who didn't actually exist! In a similar fashion, Drummond and Cauty's use of a variety of names for their musical projects made the listener question traditional notions of authorship.

From 1985 onwards, propaganda began circulating amongst the avant-garde for an Art Strike, during which cultural workers would stop producing and selling any product. Drummond and Cauty's 1992 decision not to release any more records echoes these demands and provides another example of how they've taken ideas developed on the margins of contemporary culture and used them to great effect within the pop mainstream.

Returning to the K Foundation adverts, we can see that they make perfect sense when viewed in the light of the avant-garde tradition that runs from Futurism at the beginning of this century through to groups such as the Neoists and the London Psychogeographical Association in the eighties and nineties. The ultimate meaning of the K Foundation's slogan 'ABANDON ALL ART NOW' is little different from that of 'DEMOLISH SERIOUS CULTURE', a formulation much used by the Art Strikers. As I've already said, the avant-garde has always been concerned with criticising institutionalised art.

As one would expect, much of the press reacted with utter incomprehension to the K Foundation's brilliantly conceived campaign. Charles Nevin, writing in the *Independent On Sunday*, described the advertisements as 'screamingly obscure'. Susannah Herbert and Victoria Combe, reporting for the *Daily Telegraph*, spoke of the K Foundation being 'incapable of reckoning the year correctly'. Robert Sandall, in the *Sunday Times*, suggested that the campaign 'served no obvious purpose other than to fritter away about £70,000'.

Several articles have stressed the fact that Drummond and Cauty have no recorded product available. This is not actually true, since much of the KLF output is readily available as American, German and Japanese imports. Likewise, the supposedly suppressed *1987* LP can be obtained easily enough in its original form as a bootleg. However, even if there was actually no product available at the retail end of the trade, the ads could still generate income for Drummond and Cauty because publishing remains the most lucrative area of the music business for major acts. Apart from anything else, the K Foundation campaign has exposed the pundits who've suggested the ads are economically unviable as being completely ignorant of how the entertainment industry operates and what constitutes effective advertising.

Meanwhile, a *Guardian* article by-lined to John Ezard, called the K Foundation Award a 'hoax'. This description is utterly misconceived. From a financial perspective, the K Foundation Award is considerably more substantial than the Turner Prize. Rather than questioning the validity of Drummond and Cauty's activities, anyone with a modicum of intelligence will see the intervention as a means of deflating the value of prizes awarded by bureaucratic institutions for what a bunch of suits imagine to be individual creative excellence! The K Foundation campaign functions on numerous levels but the so called quality press appears incapable of comprehending this.

And so, Drummond and Cauty are succeeding in another of their stated aims, which is to 'divide and kreate'. The pundits who find the K Foundation ads 'confusing' clearly belong among the ranks of reactionaries. Those who see the campaign as a remarkable manifestation of the contemporary avant-garde, will no doubt join the growing band of individuals who wish to build a new culture, so that they can live in a world of ever-growing ecstasy.

First published in *G-Spot* 9, Winter '93.

The avant-garde and fictional excess

I'D LIKE TO START BY DEALING with the fact that Rachel Whiteread won the Turner Prize earlier this week. Although this might not be of much interest to authors of literary fiction, as will become clear during the course of this talk, I'm a representative of the avant-garde and as such I'm not going to limit myself to commenting on a single creative medium.

No one should be surprised that Whiteread won the Turner Prize. It was, from the start, highly unlikely that Bow Neighbourhood would rescind the demolition order on Whiteread's 'sculpture' *House*[1]. Awarding Whiteread the prize was the art establishment's way of putting the screws on Tower Hamlets council. There are numerous factions within the power structure of our society and it is only natural that the culturally dominant section of the 'bourgeoisie' should see the awarding of arts prizes as a means of placing pressure on their political brethren. Similar considerations led to Salman Rushdie being awarded the Booker of Bookers in October.

As someone who had the misfortune to live a few doors up from Whiteread's 'sculpture' during the mid-eighties, I'm in a position to state categorically that the furore surrounding the demolition has nothing to do with the real issues raised by *House*. The sculpture is certainly an example of imperialism, if the term is understood in the way Henry Flynt used it during the mid-sixties. Although largely written out of cultural history, Flynt was the driving force behind conceptual art. However, he soon abandoned activity of this type and instead, set up the group Action Against Cultural Imperialism to picket concerts by the chauvinist composer Karlheinz Stockhausen.

On the *Without Walls* TV coverage of the Turner Prize, Whiteread described *House* as being typical of the Victorian housing that is found all over London. In fact, this is not even true of the structure's architecture. In the East End, the larger Victorian homes tend to be located to the north, well away from the docks. Whiteread's desire to 'universalise' the meaning of this particular terrace, results in the building being stripped of it's history and the deep political implications of that history.

Until very recently, the space *House* occupies formed a part of a terraced row that was bomb damaged during the war and condemned in 1946. The fact that people were still living in these condemned buildings more than forty-five years later, tells us a great deal about London's on-going housing shortage. When I moved into the terrace, there was immense confusion about who owned the houses. The Greater London Council had just been abolished and neither the local council nor the Parks Authority wanted to take responsibility for these former GLC homes.

Housing is a particularly explosive issue in Tower Hamlets, which has the largest concentration of council tenants in the country. As a result, council seats are contested almost entirely on the basis of housing policy. The ruling Liberal Party's housing allocations procedure has been the subject of repeated criticism by the Commission for Racial Equality. Undoubtedly, policies such as the 'Sons and Daughters' scheme, helped create the climate in which British National Party candidate Derek Beackon was able to win a council seat on the Isle of Dogs.[2]

Although Whiteread's intentions are primarily aesthetic, she simultaneously smothers a vast range of political issues and instead attempts to 'reveal something previously unknown' (*Sunday Times Magazine* 14/11/93). In effect, *House* robs those who once lived in Grove Road of their own past, replacing it with a supposedly 'higher set of values'. As I've already pointed out, when all is said and done, this is imperialism.[3]

In January 1987, about a year before Whiteread began making her casts, I satirised the art world in a story called *Straight*. In this piece, written and published before Whiteread began the series of works that have made her famous, one of the many 'fictional' examples of moronically stupid artistic activity was a pair of sculptors who made plaster casts of rocks.[4]

At the beginning of this year, I wrote a novel partially set in the terraced row of which *House* was once a part. I wasn't interested in universalising the situation I'd encountered there in the mid-eighties, I wanted to deal with specifics. The response from most of those in the book trade was astounding. The book, *Red London*, was considered too original to be published, too specialised &c. Likewise, while some publishers told me my work was too left-wing, the 'marxist' Neil Belton – who currently holds the Editor Of

The Year Award – complained that the way I deal with class is 'a next-door neighbour to Strasserism'. But then Belton is a fanatical nationalist and so it is hardly surprising that he attempts to smear anyone who uses class analysis, while simultaneously attempting to pass himself off as a 'radical' because he supports the Irish bourgeoisie against what he mistakenly perceives as a monolithic English nation.

Contrary to the perceptions of the narrow minded 'professionals' who run the publishing industry, I'm not interested in belonging to either the left or the right – and I've said elsewhere that in a hundred years time, the terms communism and fascism will be as meaningless to the average person as Guelph and Ghibelline. But to me, it would have been absurd to set a novel in a long condemned and now demolished terrace in Tower Hamlets and then not make any reference to the way in which housing was such a contentious issue within local politics.

While a work such as *House* would result in a building being stripped of its specific history wherever it was realised, it is telling that Whiteread should choose to make this work in Tower Hamlets in 1993. And despite Whiteread's intentions, what's interesting about both *House* and the Turner Prize, is what went on outside them. This year, a series of press and television adverts alerted the public to the existence of the K Foundation Award for the worst body of artistic work produced over the previous twelve months. Rachel Whiteread won both the K Foundation Award and Turner Prize on the 23rd November.

Meanwhile, in the *Times*, Richard Cork was given half a page to berate 'Britain's perennially begrudging attitude to the avant-garde' on Turner Prize day. Among other things, Cork defended Whiteread's reactionary work *House* as 'an austere yet melancholy monument'. Neither Whiteread nor Picasso, who Cork also 'defends' in his piece, are actually members of the avant-garde. As Peter Burger points out in his book *The Theory of the Avant-Garde*, avant-gardism entails a critique of the institution of art – whereas Whiteread and Picasso enjoy an unproblematic relationship with the art world.

On Tuesday, the avant-garde wasn't to be seen at the Turner Prize gathering, it was to be found among that select band of individuals who'd organised the K Foundation's attack on the smug complacency of the arts establishment. Thanks to the adverts Bill Drummond and Jimmy Cauty placed around the *Without Walls* TV coverage of the Turner Prize ceremony, 'dignitaries' such as Lord Polumbo were revealed as buffoons. While Polumbo ranted about the dunces who attack cultural innovations, his rhetoric showed him to be a complete idiot.[5] Polumbo claimed that there are no monuments erected to critics and presented himself as a champion of progressive culture, while ignoring the fact that it was critics who picked the winner of the prize he was awarding.

It is the K Foundation, rather than Whiteread, who represent a vital and innovative strand within contemporary culture. Their work is simultaneously a critique and a celebration of 'consumer capitalism'. Above all, what's enjoyable is the gusto with which they attack the self-righteous bureaucrats who pretend to be the guardians of our culture. I've been working along similar lines for the past decade, hopefully this is evident in the following extract from a story entitled *New Britain.*

> McKane made the girl spread her arms against a wall of the Mary Ward Centre. He took a pair of handcuffs from his pocket and slipped them over Lisa's wrists, which were now held directly above her head. Then the young anarchist pulled down O'Brien's leggings, so that her arse was exposed to the jeering crowd. Hamish lifted an open palm up into the air before bringing it down against the girl's naked flesh. This was the signal his comrades had been waiting to receive before launching their assault on Crud House. Dozens of windows shattered as bricks and petrol bombs rained against the building. Within seconds, Crud House had disappeared beneath a sheet of flame.
>
> 'Old farts out!' the crowd chanted in unison. 'We want books full of sex, violence and anarcho-sadism, not boring literary crap in which nothing happens!' [6]

The avant-garde desire to criticise the institution of art, in this case a conservative publishing house, should be readily evident in the passage I've just read. With a few notable exceptions, British literary critics have difficulty dealing with writing of this type. This is not just because it attacks the enervated style of literature they generally praise. The idea of appropriating pulp narrative and critically applying this fictional technique in the production of literature, is fundamentally alien to our culture, although it has been common in France since the advent of Surrealism.

In this country, it is not only critics who are flummoxed by the literary innovations introduced by Lautreamont during the nineteenth-century and later taken up by the Surrealists. Among the handful of English writers who've seen fit to champion Lautreamont's prose, most have failed miserably in their attempts to draw inspiration from his work. A typical example is Jeremy Reed, who is hung up on all the details of decadence but has failed to grasp its essence. Lautreamont wrote that he would leave no memoirs, Reed has written a fictional autobiography of his hero.

Lautreamont drew critically upon the popular fiction published in the decades before he set to work on *Maldoror*, and his English followers have attempted to imitate this style. It should go without saying that this is a pointless exercise. While acknowledging the influence of Lautreamont, in their own novels the Surrealists tended to draw upon more contemporary works, such as the remarkably successful *Fantomas* series. Likewise, when I decided to write fiction of this type, I drew on the youth culture novels I'd read when I was at school – such as Richard Allen's *Skinhead* and Mick Norman's *Guardian Angels* – rather than setting out to imitate the prose of Lautreamont and later writers of the yellow nineties.

Moving on, there are other influences in the passage I've just read that prove problematic to British critics, because they are unfamiliar with them. Although dejargonised and rendered in the language of pulp fiction, the influence of anti-Oedipal theorists such as Klaus Theweleit is at work here. Take the lines: 'the weight of the anarchist pressing down against her, gave the girl a sense of security. In a situation such as this, she knew exactly where to find the boundaries that marked the limits of her being.' Although applied to a female masochist rather than a male soldier, I'm making use of Theweleit's ideas of the fascist personality being produced by a simultaneous fear of ego dissolution and belief in violence as a means of fulfilling an alienated longing for fusion and explosion of the ego boundary.

Apart from continental theory, another device I've adopted for deconstructing fictional forms is the use of repetition. The depiction of sex and violence in my work is both ritualised and rationalised. This is something that seems to have caused British publishers and critics endless trouble, from de Sade on downwards. In my case, violence is more often that not described using a phrase I lifted from Peter Cave's novel *Mama*: 'the bastard staggered backwards spitting out gouts of blood and the occasional piece of broken tooth'.

The treatment of sex is only slightly more subtle, and is an attempt to push tendencies common in pulp fiction to an extreme. Where a genuine hack will talk of their protagonists losing control of their bodies during sex, I describe 'million year old genetic codes being scrambled and unscrambled across the muscular structure' of this or that bulk. I also resort to talk of 'mudflats' and 'a DNA encoded replay of the first star exploding'. Repetition of this type reminds the reader of the fictive nature of the narrative and provides a means of exploring the bizarre ways in which much popular fiction treats sex and violence as both mechanical and mystical.

Reversal is another trick I use to explore the construction of sexual stereotypes. So, for example, after a pulp cliché such as describing a woman as having 'curves in all the right places', I will then apply a similar formula to a male character and say he has 'bulges in all the right places'. Hopefully, it's now clear that I'm interested in fiction as a mode of discourse and completely reject nineteenth-century ideas about 'characterisation' and 'literary depth'. This will be apparent in the following extract from a story called *Grrrl Power*, which parodies media coverage of the riot grrrl movement:

> As the band sped through the opening bars, there was a disturbance at the door. The bouncers were overwhelmed and a gang of grrrls dressed in leather jackets and DMs raced into the pub wielding baseball bats. The amazons attack went unopposed as they charged into the room. The sheer unexpectedness of the assault gave them a massive psychological advantage. The crowd parted as if it was the sea responding to a command from Moses. The wimmin were like a whirlwind, scattering blokes in their wake. Robin Rolls reached the stage and whacked Phil Moronic over the head with her bat. The singer slumped to the floor, knocked for six by a single blow. The music ground to a halt as the sisters smashed guitars and amps. The drummer ran through a side exit and thereby escaped the righteous blows of the Valerie Solanas Commando and their crew – but his kit was trashed in retaliation.
>
> 'Death to boy rock!' someone shouted through a microphone. [7]

It should be apparent from the passage I've just read, that one of the things I've adopted from pulp books of the past twenty or so years, is a prose style modelled on tabloid journalism. I've no time for the leaden sentences of Martin Amis and his imitators. I much prefer the direct approach of a metaphor like 'the crowd parted as if it was the sea responding to a command from Moses', to long winded efforts along the lines of: 'the hall smelled of boiling cabbage – or, let's be accurate, it smelled as if someone had eaten six bushels of asparagus, washed down with as many quarts of Guinness, and pissed over the walls, ceiling and floor.'

Amis goes to great lengths to draw attention to what he perceives to be his own cleverness. But the first part of sentence I've just quoted is cancelled out by what follows, and any hack worth his or her salt would have crossed it out.[8] I want to explore the ways in which narrative fiction is constructed and the use of clichés such as 'anger rising like bile from the pit of his stomach' or 'like moths to a flame, junkies to a fix', are by far the best way to do this. Another problem I have with literary fiction is that the lengthy sentences become overburdened with words and the resultant prose lacks any sense of rhythm.

I prefer works that are conceptually, rather than verbally, overloaded. The following passage ought to illustrate this, while showing once again the ways in which I've drawn on Theweleit's theories. I begin by sounding plausible, then funny, and finally descend into a hell of expressionist madness characterised by semantic confusion. Conflicting ideologies are heated until meltdown is achieved. The result is a humorous revelation of the fact that 'left' and 'right' wing doctrines are distorted reflections of each other. This is hardly surprising given the fact that communism and fascism ultimately spring from a single source – Hegel.

I'm not in the business of offering political cure-alls – but I've got a few suggestions about improving British books. Some people rather simplisticly imagine that I want to replace literature with pulp fiction. In fact, I'd rather create something unprecedented from a marriage of these two antagonistic forms. Anyway, this is the key passage from a novel called *Defian Pose*:[9]

> Parliament Square was a riot of colour and action. Flames were leaping from Big Ben and Westminster Abbey. The trouble had spread down Millbank and word had just reached those at the epicentre of the disturbances that the Tate Gallery had been fired. The news that billions of pounds' worth of modern art was going up in smoke, brought loud cheers from the crowd. As street hardened proletarians they understood the oppressive function of bourgeois culture. They were going to build a new world without art or any of the other elitist garbage that characterised the reigning society. It goes without saying that quick-thinking militants had wreaked similar destruction on the National Gallery, the ICA and the numerous palaces and foreign embassies located in the area liberated by the insurgents.

Footnotes (added between December 93 and February 94)

1 What Whiteread actually did, was to propose that a terraced house scheduled for demolition be filled with concrete and then that the brickwork of the original structure be prised away. This project, carried out by a team of workmen and sponsored by huge corporations, was then glorified with the title HOUSE and described as 'sculpture'.

If, as is sometimes asserted by cultural reactionaries, the task of the artist is to give representation to the unconscious, Whiteread has succeeded admirably. Houses are traditionally considered a symbol of the unconscious and by filling a terrace with concrete, Whiteread showed herself to be intellectually, creatively and emotionally blocked – something that is evident in all her 'work'.

193 Grove Road, the site of *House*, had previously been occupied by Sidney Gale, a retired docker. The terraced row in which Mr Gale lived for most of his life was demolished because the houses were in very poor condition. The pensioner resisted eviction, even after the other homes in the block had been knocked down. As was reported in the *London Psychogeographical Association Newsletter* No. 5, Sidney Gale's terrace stood alone for months, shored up with scaffolding and placards declaring 'This is my home, I live here'.

This cheerful reminder of popular resistance to bureaucracy was swooped upon by Whiteread – who made no mention of Mr Gale in her publicity material. In much the same way that Christian churches were frequently placed on Pagan sites in order to neutralise them, so artists take over symbols of resistance as a means of sanitising them. Art 'critics' are then employed to rewrite history in a truly Orwellian style. For an example of this, see the *Up Front* piece by Simon Jenkins in *Modern Painters* Winter 93, where the author blatantly lies about how 'Whiteread secured a stay of execution' on 193 Grove Road. Whiteread's *House* was finally demolished on 11/1/94, more than two months behind schedule.

2 The 'Sons and Daughters' scheme made the allocation of council properties to the adult offspring of existing tenants a priority, in effect, favouring 'white' applicants for housing.

3 The fact that after Bow Neighbourhood announced *House* would be demolished, Whiteread suddenly took to claiming her work was some vague and

apparently 'universal' protest against homelessness, doesn't alter the fact that artists are the real philistines.

4 This story also foreshadows the work of the K Foundation, amongst others. The *Melody Maker* (4/12/93), reported that the K Foundation had produced a series of 'art works' that consisted of money nailed to pieces of wood, and that these were to be sold for half the value of the cash they contained. The following press statement was also quoted: 'Over the years the face value will be eroded by inflation. While the artistic value (due to the works' position in the amended History of Art) will rise and rise. The precise point at which the artistic value will overtake the face value is unknown. De-construct the work now and you double your money. Hang it on a wall and watch the face value erode, the market value fluctuate, and the artistic value soar. The choice is yours.'
Straight features a character called Ken Knobb who gets a nurse to perform enemas on him as works of performance art. He then holds lotteries to sell test-tubes of his shit. The winner of the lottery has to choose whether they want money or Knobb's excrement as their prize: 'I'd like those of you who've placed a stake in this lottery to think about the difficult choice you may have to make. First, consider that inflation will reduce the value of the money, while my shit will increase in value. Secondly, consider the fact that the shit will degrade. If my excrement is to retain it's value, money has to be spent on having it preserved, whereas the thirty-seven quid could be invested for a quick profit.' (*Straight* included in *Smile* 10, London 1987 – reprinted in *No Pity*, AK Press, Edinburgh 1993, where this extract can be found on page 74).

5 Several people have already pointed out that Polumbo was unable to correctly name Van Goth's art dealer brother.

6 *No Pity* (AK Press Edinburgh 1993) pages 137 to 138. The actual passage read during the talk was longer and ran from the middle of page 137 to the top of page 139.

7 *No Pity* (AK Press Edinburgh 1993) page 16. The actual passage read during the talk was longer and ran from the top of page 16 to the top of page 17.

8 To labour the point, 'worth his or her salt' is exactly the type of verbal short-cut a hack would use.

9 *Defiant Pose* (Peter Owen, London 1991) page 132. The actual passage read during the talk was longer and ran from page 132 to page 136.

From orgasm to obliteration

IN MY FICTION, I use a technique known as the plot thins, what I'm saying is that I've adopted the easiest way of resolving what happens to my characters as a story progresses, which is to kill them off. Death gives a finality to the fate of the 'individuals' who people my plots. When someone snuffs it, there's no loose ends for the reader to worry about. This may sound crass but then I'm not interested in traditional notions of characterisation and literary depth. In any case, the central character in most of my writing isn't an 'individual', it's London.

The reason I write about London is that it's both familiar and exciting. The English capital provides a dynamic urban environment forever in the throes of transformation. Although I often dream and write about destroying whole swathes of the city, in the end the place is like Dracula, it can't die. The millions who pass through the West End and give the area it's sense of urgency are subject to psychic breakdown and death, but the backdrop against which they act out their petty dramas is seemingly stable in its state of constant flux.

One of the things that plays on my mind as I write about London, is the fact that it has no centre. The City and Westminster are it's two most important hubs, having rivalled each other for nearly a thousand years. I have a very strong sense of the zones that make up the sprawling metropolis as I move through its streets. Travelling on the underground doesn't obliterate these differences, it simply sharpens the shock of moving from one zone to another. Ambling along London's numerous waterways probably provides the most gentle means of experiencing the sharp contrasts between the variegated zones that make up the city.

The piece I'm going to recite begins with a riot in Parliament Square, where several examples of architecture that weigh us down with too great a sense of history are wiped from the face of London. Then the main protagonists take to the Thames in a rowing boat and the city's famous bridges are used as markers on a journey to the east. An alternative history is called up along the way, a chronicle of dissent on the part of the oppressed. The hero undergoes psychic breakdown as the price he must pay for acting as a cipher through which various oppositional currents can pass. At the cataclysmic conclusion, this character moves from the ecstasies of orgasm to the icy numbness of catatonic obliteration.

'Parliament Square was a riot of colour and action….' and so on from pages 132 to 136 of Defiant Pose (Peter Owen, London 1991).

Introduction for a reading at Winterschool, Glasgow, 6/1/94.

Reflections on silence

ONE OF THE FEATURES ANARCHISM shares with much 'marxist' thought, is the inability of it's adherents to deal sensibly with cultural issues. Most marxists defend one form or another of 'serious culture' because they recognise that the arts play an important role in legitimating the power of so called 'revolutionary states'. In terms of rhetoric, anarchists tend to be more 'critical' of 'serious culture' than 'marxists'. However, simply sprinkling deeply reactionary cultural activities with a handful of 'radical' words, is enough to reduce most 'revolutionaries' to silence.

Given that the Anarcho-Situationist milieu produces virtually no films whatsoever, it's extraordinary that Isaac Cronin and Terrel Seltzer's videotape *Call It Sleep* (1982), has circulated for years without the inflated claims the duo make for this work being widely refuted. Cronin and Seltzer have stated that: *Call It Sleep* is the first visual work produced in the United States which makes use of the Situationist technique of detournement'. This assertion is patently absurd, since detournement as practised by the Situationist International entailed the meaning of the appropriated material being subverted. Translated literally, 'detournement' means 'diversion'! In stark contrast to this, Cronin and Seltzer simply string together various pieces of tv footage as illustrations for the ritualised denunciations of 'capitalism' that have been dubbed onto the soundtrack of their film. In fact, the function of these clips is identical to that of 'degenerate' painting in the infamous 'decadent art' exhibitions organised by the nazis. Thus, it is hardly surprising that Cronin and Seltzer use a soundtrack of pop songs to accompany the worst examples of 'degenerate' culture, while classical music underscores their 'insights' into the nature of contemporary society.

Likewise, one of the four sections of the film is dedicated to *The Cadre*, a figure subjected to extreme abuse whose depiction parallels the way in which nazi propagandists scapegoated Jews. Another section of *Call It*

Sleep is given over to a completely outdated fixation with Bolshevism. Here, Cronin and Seltzer cross Situationist ideas with right-wing hysteria about 'Reds'. We're told that a bolshevik was the 'founding father of modern cinema' – and presumably the 'Spectacle' as well! There's no mention of D. W. Griffith, who could just as well be granted this 'accolade'. Perhaps this director's brand of 'hooded Americanism' is so uncomfortably close to Cronin and Seltzer's right-wing Situationism that it can't be acknowledged.

Call It Sleep is not a visual work, its 'message' is hammered home via the soundtrack. The authoritarian male voice that drones on for much of the film's 42 minutes might as well belong to 'God', because 'He' tells us the meaning of everything we're shown. As such, the videotape is an example of totalitarian art, the audience is expected to consume the work passively and without thought. The film is a propaganda exercise and its content is of little consequence. What matters to Cronin and Seltzer is that we uncritically accept their messages, even when these contradict each other. At the beginning of the video, they claim that 'everyone drives the same cars, takes the same drugs, sees the same movies, reads the same pop thinkers'. This is contradicted later on when the 'Cadre' are depicted as consuming different books and pop thinkers to ordinary workers (thus confirming their 'alien' status as 'rootless cosmopolitans'). If *Call It Sleep* was a successful example of totalitarian art, it's message would envelope the audience and these changes of tack would be smoothly accomplished – the wheels in our heads being turned first one way, and then the other, without us even noticing any 'inexplicable' reversals. The fact that the film has made no impact beyond Anarcho-Situationist circles, demonstrates that it fails as a piece of propaganda. It is technically, as well as conceptually, inept.

The stew of Situationist and 'right-wing' 'individualist' ideas from which Cronin and Seltzer's work sprang, also nurtured the so called 'marginal milieu'. Although these self-styled 'impossibilists' regularly voice their opposition to 'serious culture', they take their name from the marginal arts, an umbrella term for activities such as 'intermedia' and 'networking'. Probably the best known 'marginal' is Michael Tolson, who also works under the names Tim Ore and tENTATIVELY a cONVENIENCE. Despite Tolson's protests that he is not 'an artist', his activities lie in a direct line of descent from the 'weak' avant-garde traditions of John Cage and Fluxus.[1]

As well as being the leading 'marginal', Tolson played a significant role in the Neoist Network. His patently false claim that Neoism was a prefix and a suffix without a content, is rooted in a Cagean obsession with 'emptiness'. Tolson's desire to portray Neoist Apartment Festivals as 'open situations', is indicative of his status as a failed avant-gardist.. As such, he is unwilling to admit that Neoist events precluded the active participation of anyone unfamiliar with the weak 'avant-gardism' of Fluxus and Mail Art. This fanciful denial of his aesthetic roots, renders Tolson's work inaccessible to anyone outside the 'marginal milieu'. In other words, like most artists, Tolson is wilfully obscure.

The Cagean roots of both Neoism and the 'marginals' are readily evident in a text Tolson produced during the early eighties entitled *Sayings Of A Famous Artist*. This short piece exposes the artistic mind-set of the 'marginal milieu' through the attraction it betrays towards tautological formulas that sound profound but lack any empirical content.[2] Tolson baldly asserts that to be 'famous' , one has to be 'recognisable' and that repetition is a short cut to this state of affairs. He concludes this piece of chicanery by claiming that he's made 'a clear and blatant exposure of some fame mechanisms'. Tolson simply ignores the fact that to be 'recognisable' in terms of art historical discourse, one is by definition 'famous'. What he offers as an insight into the mechanisms of fame is actually a blatant mystification of how the culture industry operates. Appearances of repetition within an oeuvre can only be observed by 'the public' after the 'individual' responsible for the works in question has become 'famous' and thus 'recognisable'. For this to happen, a consortium of galleries, critics, collectors and museums must spot in any given artist's work a break with (and/or a continuation) of a 'recognisable' 'tradition'.

Artists don't make themselves famous, there is a strict division of labour within the cultural field and fame entails the active collaboration of numerous 'individuals' and institutions. Tolson, like the producers of *Call It Sleep*, is insignificant. His work is largely unknown outside the 'marginal'/anarchist scene, and this is just one mark of its failure. What's telling, is the critical silence and mindless enthusiasm with which self-styled 'revolutionaries' greet works such as *Call It Sleep*. Cultural productions of this type ought to be subjected to merciless criticism, since they are even more reactionary than the garbage spewed out by the arts establishment.

Commissioned by the Belgian magazine *Perspectief* in late 1993 for a special issue dedicated to 'art and anarchism', it is not known whether the piece was ever run.

Footnotes

1. While the title of this essay is intended as an echo of Sorel's *Reflections On Violence*, with regard to Tolson, it might just as well be a play on Cage's first collection of articles, *Silence*. Tolson shares with Cage a delight in a 'beat' version of 'Zen' that finds silence 'profound'.

2. Likewise, Tolson's obsession with the 'commodification' of culture is a mark of his inability to understand art's ideological function. He seems to think that the ruling class values art because of the price tag individual pieces of it carry, when this is merely a distorted reflection of its simultaneous use as both a means of social integration and class distinction, as well as the ability of 'serious culture' to satisfy the 'mystical' longings of a certain type of individual who has abandoned more traditional modes of religious belief. Intellectual failure of this type explains why many of those belonging to the 'marginal milieu' equate 'progressive' tendencies in culture with financial hardship, thus reinforcing the absurd myth of the impoverished artist starving in a garret, and simultaneously missing much that is subversive in popular entertainment.

Up! up! and away!

Levitating the Pavilion Theatre and other scams

THE HISTORY OF THE AVANT-GARDE is a history of buffoonery, consequently most of those who attempt to take the tradition seriously end up looking like idiots. Nevertheless, from Situationism to the Art Strike, those involved with Neo-Dadaist Retro-Futurism have conducted their pranks with enormous solemnity. Anti-institutional activism thrives on contradiction and the greatest strength of oppositional culture is concealed in the fact that the various individuals pursuing it are willing to expend an enormous amount of energy on what appear to be extremely trivial activities.

Because a key element of the avant-garde's praxis is opposition to the institution of art, the elite operating at the cutting edge of culture must necessarily do so in a way that resembles the work of advertising agencies. The avant-garde cannot rely on the traditional mechanisms of the culture industry for publicity because it operates outside them. It is for this reason that the founding document of the tradition, the first *Futurist Manifesto*, was originally published as a paid advert in a national newspaper.

Pranks are often used to draw attention to areas of contention within culture and the figure of the trickster has long been familiar to us, but the single-minded zeal with which the avant-garde pursues its stunts differentiates such activities from older traditions. While the trickster is generally invoked as a means of restoring traditional values when social conflicts have thrown the world out of kilter, the task the avant-garde sets itself is the symbolic overthrow of the old order.

The beliefs of those who fear change, and those who advocate it, are often mirror images of each other. To exploit this state of affairs, in March 1993 I set up the Neoist Alliance, with a six point programme loosely modelled on *The Plan of the Jews* written by the notorious anti-Semite Arnold Leese in 1934. What Leese denigrated as the strategy of those who opposed fascism, I adopted as a positive programme. The name of my group was, of course, intended to be confusing, it has nothing whatsoever to do with the Neoist Network of the nineteen-eighties.

The first public activity undertaken by the Neoist Alliance was a rally in the City Of London on 1 May 1993 to celebrate the 217th anniversary of the founding of the Illuminati by Adam Weishaupt in Bavaria. Although this passed without any media interest, it served to establish the Neoist Alliance as having taken up the torch of progress and enlightenment passed down through the Templars, the Rosicrucians, the Illuminati, the League of the Just, the Society of Seasons, The Club of the Pantheon, the Committee of Equals, the Society of Flowers and the Situationist International.

Two weeks later, the Neoist Alliance was picketing a Stockhausen concert at the Pavilion Theatre in Brighton. This was one of four protests taking place in Brighton on 15 May and the only one to get coverage in the local press. With it, I succeed in bringing various subversive elements from the past back into play. To an extent, the rally was a re-run of Action Against Cultural Imperialism's 1964 New York picket of Stockhausen at the Judson Hall. But I'd also sent out a press release saying the Neoist Alliance would be levitating the Pavilion Theatre, an idea lifted from the Yippies anti-Vietnam war protest outside the Pentagon in Washington.

My mix and match approach to the political happening works because most people lack a historical grounding in the activities of the counter-culture, and so what might appear hackneyed to those familiar with the source material, seems fresh and bizarre to everyone else. And the protest certainly hit the wrong note with the pretentious high flyers who'd organised the Stockhausen recital. Art bores really hate being criticised by individuals more culturally advanced than themselves, especially when humour is used to make a 'serious' point!

The arts magazine *Hybrid* (No. 3, June/July 93), turned up to review the Stockhausen concert, but covered my picket instead. Quoting a point from the Neoist Alliance programme, they said that 'someone, somewhere, has been here before'. However, the reviewer was unable to identify the entire platform as being plagiarised from Arnold Leese. Clearly, the knowing tone *Hybrid* adopted about the Neoist Alliance was simply a bluff, since they were unable to name the 'original' sources for anything we said or did in Brighton.

The Neoist Alliance chose the literary establishment as its next target. The avant-garde has always employed scandal as a propaganda weapon because this is one way of transgressing the limits imposed on institutionalised culture. With this end in mind, I circulated a leaflet that announced a psychic attack on the book trade, timed as a celebration of the first anniversary of the suicide of 'highbrow' novelist Richard Burns. This was considered sick by many of the bozos who work in publishing, and thereby exposed the ways in which the cultural establishment uses notions of good taste to exclude individuals, ideas and opinions from its 'charmed' ranks.

Within days of this occult attack on the publishing industry, Martin Amis left his wife, Salman Rushdie was whinging in the *Guardian* about British politicians ignoring his plight, and something so horrible had happened to Julian Barnes, that the media dared not report it for fear of being sued for libel. And this was after I'd given advance notice of my plans and the book trade had hired numerous psychics to organise a defence against the magickal onslaught!

My next tactic against the literary establishment was to distribute fake Booker Prize invitations to down and outs. Fleet Street chose to ignore the fact that this was done under the aegis of the Neoist Alliance and reported it as an act of sabotage perpetrated by a 'fed-up author'. I followed this up, by submitting a piece of my own work for the *Literary Review* Grand Booby Prize for Bad Sex in Fiction. Lacking a sense of humour, Auberon Waugh disqualified my entry despite the fact that there had been nothing in the announcement of the award banning an author from entering his or her own work. Melvyn Bragg won the prize, demonstrating yet again how things have been stitched up by literary insiders who are quite prepared to cheat and change rules as they go along, in order to prevent those they don't want within their 'charmed' circle from gatecrashing the party!

Bill Drummond and Jimmy Cauty, formerly of the KLF and now active as the K Foundation, upstaged the Turner Prize last year by awarding forty thousand pounds to the winner for producing the worst body of art over the previous twelve months. Without doubt, the prank succeeded in satirising the institution of art, but the K Foundation failed to explain the ways in which the winner's work was imperialist. It was therefore left to the Neoist Alliance to issue a leaflet attacking Rachel Whiteread and her 'sculpture' House. In this, I explained that Whiteread's desire to 'universalise' the meaning of the terrace she'd transformed into a concrete cast, resulted in the building being stripped of its history and the deep political implications of that history.

The K Foundation publicised their prank with a series of press and television adverts. Their amply financed activities received a good deal more press coverage than the avant-garde has generally gardened in recent years. Although stunts don't bag column inches in direct proportion to the amount of money spent on them, a prank with a publicist orchestrating the coverage is likely to do better than something executed on a shoe-string budget.

Since the avant-garde wishes to get its criticisms of the institution of art across to as many people as possible, it makes sense to spend money on a press officer. I'd have hired Mick Houghton to publicise my pranks if I'd been able to afford him. Most of those criticising the KLF (see, for example, the *NME* letters page of 11/12/93), hadn't grasped the mechanisms by which the culture industry operates and thus failed to understand the K Foundation's activities as a contemporary articulation of the avant-garde critique of the institution of art.

What's particularly interesting about Drummond and Cauty is the way they've taken ideas from the avant-garde of the 1980s and injected them into mainstream culture. I said in a lecture at the V&A last January that the KLF would be used to validate the Neoist, Plagiarist and Art Strike movements in the same way that the historical standing of the Situationist International had been boosted by critics citing their alleged influence on the Sex Pistols. Given Drummond and Cauty's present activities as the K Foundation, the connections between them and the eighties avant-garde are much closer than the rather tenuous links made between Guy Debord and Johnny Rotten. A long term campaign to exploit this state of affairs is my avant-garde version of *The Great Rock 'N' Roll Swindle*' it's a prank that will hopefully overshadow the quickie stunts I was pulling last year.

Notes for a lecture at Winterschool, Glasgow, 4/1/94

Strategies of writing

WRITING IN THE OBSERVER of 3/4/94, Elizabeth Young outlined two traditions in post-war American fiction. One is the academically based, 'creative' writing school work of Saul Bellow and John Updike. The other is influenced by the Beat Generation, nourished by contact with the European avant-garde and typified by the work of William Burroughs. Young identified this second current in its contemporary incarnation as transgressive fiction. I even got a name check because I'm one of the few British writers included in the second *High Risk* anthology.

Young reviewed my first two novels in the *New Statesman* of 10/5/91, where she declared that I was 'a writer with a profound commitment to intertextuality'. I'd agree, and therefore feel free to quote someone whose work I've never read. According to Dr. Johnson: 'No man but a blockhead ever wrote, except for money'. I've seen this declaration used in several pieces of journalism in recent months. If by a blockhead, Johnson meant those bozos who simply want to be recognised as great writers and don't care whether or not their work has any effect on the world, then I am in complete agreement with him. However, I'm more interested in treating writing as a game than a way of making a living, the devaluation and re-use of elements from the past within my texts creates a labyrinth in which the reader can 'aimlessly' drift, only to be drawn forward by a carefully selected series of signifiers. It follows from this that I'm deeply concerned about how people respond to what I do and I feel nothing but contempt for those imbeciles who think writing is an 'art' that somehow floats above social relations.

My own work emerges from within the avant-garde tradition typified by groups such as the Futurists, Dadaists and Situationists, all of whom were deeply critical of the institution of art. Therefore, I see those men and wimmin who make up the British literary establishment as a legitimate target for the odd prank that contests the hegemony of their views. The totalitarian nature of the dominant culture is illustrated by the fact that virtually all those who constitute the literary 'mafia' consider open and public criticism of Salman Rushdie taboo. Therefore, on 14 February under the auspices of the Neoist Alliance, I aimed a double whammy at this target.

Firstly, I sent a fraudulent press release headlined 'Smash the Fatwa, Burn the Koran!' to fifty literary critics. This announced that Salman Rushdie had teamed up with conceptual artist John Latham to create a protest action on the fifth anniversary of the death sentence issued against him. It claimed that Rushdie and Latham were going to burn copies of the Bible and the Koran at a secret location in London. The text concluded with a few words I'd attributed to Rushdie: 'Since going into hiding, I've been studying middle eastern history and now realise that the workers are the only people in a position to defy intransigent Islam… In 1958 when Qasim and the free officers seized power in Iraq, the workers killed the monarch and burnt the Koran. This is the kind of activity my collaboration with John Latham is designed to encourage.' This caused a huge security flap costing thousands of pounds and for several days, Special Branch were left wondering whether my mailing was part of an international plot being orchestrated against the author of the *Satanic Verses*.

Secondly, I issued a leaflet to 'celebrate the 5th anniversary of the death sentence passed on Salman Rushdie'. Beneath the headline 'FATWA' was the message 'smash Christianity, smash Islam, smash the literary establishment!' My intention was to upset those who mindlessly adhere to the values propagated by the culture industry. One issue that crops up endlessly in the press is illiteracy, there were three pages dedicated to this subject in yesterday's *Sunday Times*. This is why I stated that: 'The world of English letters will soon be destroyed. The sick 'men' of Bloomsbury swept away by authors whose 'writing' is so fresh that they don't know how to spell – and don't need to know, because the software that came with their PCs included a dictionary and a thesaurus.' This is an example of the psychological warfare I'm waging against the so called cultural 'elite', I'm seeking to undermine the literary establishment by playing on its fears, by telling those who belong to it that their worst nightmares have come true.

I concluded my leaflet with the proclamation that: 'humanity will not be happy until the last book bore is hung by the guts of the last mullah'. The tradition of writing drawn upon within British literary circles is generally so narrow that most of those whom I targeted with my leaflet were unlikely to notice that this slogan was a corruption of Diderot. This was another joke at the expense of the 'literati', as Georges Sorel noted in *The Illusions Of Progress*: 'Generally speaking, common people understand nothing of literary wiles; when they are told about 'making a cord for the last of the kings out of the entrails of priests', they literally believe that Diderot wanted to convince enlightened men about the necessity of disembowelling and strangling rulers in order to ensure the happiness of man'.[1]

From what's been said so far, it should be clear that my writing is aimed at two very different sets of readers. On the one hand, there are those who understand what I'm doing and appreciate my sense of humour; then there are the imbeciles who belong to the 'cultural' establishment, whose ignorance and stupidity are inevitably exposed by my pranks. An example of this is something I did with my second novel *Defiant Pose*, whose hero is continually being handed scraps of paper by beautiful wimmin with their phone numbers scrawled across them. There are always a few idiots who'll try dialling numbers they hear on records or come across in books because they suspect that these are real, so when I wrote *Defiant Pose*, I passed off the phone numbers of London police stations as those of my fictitious 'nymphomaniacs'.

My editor at Peter Owen got over excited while dialling these numbers and had them removed from the manuscript before the book was published. I laughed long and hard when this cretin moaned about having been berated by very hostile men while attempting to call the 'nymphos' given a 'fictional' depiction in my novel. This prick was too thick to work out that he'd been talking to desk sergeants, and obviously didn't cut it between the sheets since he wanted to remove a reference I'd made to a womun bellowing obscenities during sex, on the grounds that this was unrealistic. Fortunately, I was able to veto this absurd change.

I've passed many pleasant hours watching critics make fools of themselves while attempting to review my writing. The funniest reaction to date is that of Mark Sanderson in *Time Out* of 8/5/91. I'd included a scene in *Defiant Pose* where the hero kicks a dog to death. Sanderson provided the outraged response this deeply humorous vignette was calculated to elicit from dumb 'animal lovers', while simultaneously exposing his class prejudice by describing the main character as an 'oik'. Other reviewers of my fiction, such as David Flynt in *Divinity* (No. 6 Winter 93), are equally adept at betraying their own stupidity by looking for 'depth' in my writing, when it's patently obvious that along with every other 'post-modern' novelist, I've dispensed with nineteenth-century notions of literary value and have no interest in 'characterisation'. Flynt's attempt at criticism is particularly hilarious because he hasn't understood that I'm writing satire and have no interest in attempting to create narratives with a 'fixed meaning'.[2]

However, I do not consider all critics stupid and some are able to make very productive readings and misreadings of my work. Elizabeth Young kicked off her *New Statesman* review of my novels with the line 'Sweet Thames run softly till I end my song', which T. S. Eliot had appropriated from Spenser for use in *The Waste Land*. Young commented that it was a wonder I hadn't reused these words. I took this to be a challenge, and since I consider writing to be a game rather than a vocation, I've worked a variation on this phrase into my forthcoming novel *Red London*. Intelligent critics like Young have an important role to play in the generation of fictional narratives, since they are able to suggest new directions in which a writer may take their work, a function they share with a more numerous body of the non-professional readership.[3]

Another game I play when constructing narratives, concerns the length of time it takes to get a book published. Usually there is a gap of at least a year between a novel being completed and the text being offered for sale to the public. Since I want my fiction to appear contemporary, I have to guess at social and other changes that may take place between when I'm writing and when the work finally appears in print. With *Defiant Pose*, I correctly guessed that an English translation of Guy Debord's *Comments On The Society Of The Spectacle* would be available by the time the novel was published. As I wrote, there were plans afoot to build an office complex on the site that has long hosted the Brighton Sunday market. I assumed the development would go ahead and referred to it in my text, although ultimately the project was scrapped, thus introducing an inaccuracy into the book.

I also play with the intended 'meanings' of the texts I appropriate. For example, in *Defiant Pose*, I take words lifted from the notorious anti-Semitic forgery *The Protocols of the Elders of Zion*, and put them into the mouth of a neo-Nazi who rants about kicking dust in the eyes of the 'nationalist cattle' when in the 'original' the phrase is 'goy cattle'. By reversing the literal sense of the *Protocols* and placing the words in the mouth of a character whose world view is similar to that of the forgers who attributed this work to Jewish Elders, it becomes easier to understand anti-Semitism as a form of psychological projection. Likewise, I take the key scene from Goebbels' novel *Michael* and use it to demonstrate the way in which the same forces structure the ideology of both the 'left' and the 'right', resulting in these apparently antagonistic entities being no more than mirror images of each other. Thus a neo-Nazi leader uses the words Goebbels put into the mouth of his fictional depiction of Hitler, while a fictional anarchist is used to show that reversing their meaning does not really alter them. As slogans, 'Work, Honour, The Flag' and 'Anarchy, Slack, Polymorphous Perversity', function in an identical fashion, transforming those who attempt to understand them literally into mindless automatons.

Thus when members of the literary establishment describe my work as being either 'right' or 'left' wing, they do no more than demonstrate a strategically planned failure of their own understanding. What I'm doing is exposing the ways in which discourse structures ideology, and from this it should be clear that I have no wish to pursue any particular ideology as an end in itself. What the literary 'mafia' finds most offensive about my work is the fact that I treat 'art' and 'religion' as ideologies that function in an analogous fashion to the varied forms of political fanaticism (that is to say extremism of the so called 'left', 'right' AND 'centre'). Literature doesn't rise above social relations, it's a means of perpetrating the interests of a particular class, which is why those who speak about writing as an end in itself or as something of 'universal' significance, are often very actively engaged in using cultural activities as a means of buttressing and/or advancing their social position.

Notes for a lecture at Southampton Institute 11/4/94

Footnotes

1 As if wishing to prove me right in my use of Sorel's point, Phil Baker reviewing *High Risk Two* in the *Guardian* of 19/4/94 described me as a 'veteran of the 'Art Strike' and of the 'Hang Rushdie' campaign'. Of course, I knew it was likely that even the tiny minority of my opponents who were capable of recognising this corrupted citation would choose to misread it. This simply made it easier for me to demonstrate my point because after the event, it is

very difficult to prove whether the misreading of a text was a tactical decision or simply the result of ignorance. Regardless of this, I obtained the result I predicted. Given this state of affairs, only a proportion of my readers will be capable of judging whether or not it makes sense to apply the words of Max Stirner to my activities: 'Do I write out of love for men? No, I write because I want to procure for my thoughts an existence in the world; and, even if I foresaw that these thoughts would deprive you of your rest and your peace, even if I saw the bloodiest wars and the fall of many generations springing up from this seed of thought – I would nevertheless scatter it. Do with it what you will and can, this is your affair and does not trouble me'. Naturally, the tactics of the literary establishment are utterly predictable and work less well with each reuse, the smears spread about me are so similar to those directed against Ian Hamilton Finlay that the literati's lack of imagination and their inability to create rumours that might be believed by individuals who have actually read my work, beggars belief. (Note added 20/4/94).

2 I could give a great many examples of this type but will restrict myself to footnoting two more. In a xeroxed pamphlet entitled *History Begins Where Life Ends*, attributed to David A. Bannister, ex-Neoist Michael Tolson demonstrated the complete rigidity of his thinking by taking my statements on the Art Strike and related topics as literally as any book bore. For example, Tolson wails about my wry comment to the effect that 'I can report the Art Strike in the same triumphal fashion as the Situationist International wrote about the events of May 68'. Rather than concluding that I'm having a dig at the SI and simultaneously deconstructing the process of historification, Tolson absurdly assumes I literally want people to believe the Art Strike was the principal cause of a 60 per cent drop in art sales between 1990 and 1992..

A game I play with readers and critics is the placement of important information in footnotes. I did this most extensively in my first book *The Assault On Culture* and the ruse made several individuals who'd failed to read all the footnotes look like complete idiots. For example, the pro-situ hack Lucy Forsyth wrote to inform me that *The End Of Music* was published without the author's permission, something that I'd footnoted on page 84 of the book. After this, Forsyth's real reason for writing, to denounce me as 'a fart', came as something of a damp squib.

3. As Hegel slyly observed in the *Phenomenology of Mind*: 'We must have the conviction that it is of the nature of truth to prevail when its time has come, and that truth appears only when its time has come – and therefore never appears too early, nor ever finds that the public is not ready for it. And the individual needs public acceptance to prove the truth of what is as yet his solitary concern; he needs to see how the conviction that is as yet particular becomes general. But at this point the public must be distinguished from those who act as if they were its representatives and spokesmen. In some respects the public behaves differently from these people, even in the opposite way. When a philosophical essay is not found appealing, the public may good-naturedly ascribe the fault to itself but the others, sure of their competence, ascribe the sole fault to the author. In the public, the effect is quieter than the activity of these dead men when they bury their dead. The general level of insight now is more educated, curiosity is wide awake, and judgments are made more quickly than formerly; so the feet of them which shall carry thee out are already at the door. But from this we must often distinguish the slower effect which corrects the attention that was extorted by imposing assurances as well as disdainful reproaches: some writers find an audience only after a time, while others after a time have none any more.'

Fluxcontinuum:

the influence of Fluxus on later movements

I'D LIKE TO BEGIN BY POINTING OUT that the title I've chosen for this lecture is somewhat misleading. The whole notion of influence is deeply problematic, it's impossible to prove to what extent one cultural movement has been influenced by another, since there are so many factors affecting the development of avant-garde groups. So, rather than simply talking about groups that have been influenced by Fluxus, what I'm actually going to do is look at those movements which have emerged from within the same tradition, a set of precedents and co-developments encompassing Futurism, Dada, Surrealism, the Situationists and the New York Motherfuckers, amongst others.

A related problem, which I will not attempt to resolve here, is what actually constitutes Fluxus. I do not agree with those who say Fluxus is an ongoing concern, nor do I think that the group's life extended as far as the death of George Maciunas in 1978. In fact, by using a strict definition of the group's activities, concentrating on minimalism and iconoclasm, it's perfectly feasible to argue that the term Fluxus should be reserved for activities up to 1966. Certainly, by the time of the *Fluxshoe*, what the word was being used to describe was very different to the Wiesbaden manifestations of September 1962.

One of the things Fluxus had metamorphosed into by the early 1970s was Mail Art, sometimes called Correspondence Art or the Eternal Network. This activity had its roots in a number of diverse sources. Somewhat misleadingly, the Pop artist Ray Johnson is widely known as the father or 'grandada' of Mail Art. Johnson began his mailings in the 1940s and by the early 1960s, was using the parodic name New York Correspondence School as an umbrella term for this activity. By the early seventies, the Fluxus movement had, to an extent, merged with a number of other groups and individuals who shared Johnson's interest in aesthetic communication through the mail, thus avoiding the mediation of a gallery. Although people come and go, this Network still exists today and currently operates through the internet and faxes, as well as by the old standby of the postal system.

Mail Art can best be described as a form of picturesque interaction, sometimes artists send each other instructions for performances, sometimes xeroxed collages or merely envelopes full of junk. Much Mail Art is serial in nature and should be viewed as a kind of call and response between the various networkers who are in contact with one another. It is this process of communication that is essential to Mail Art, and a proportion of the artefacts which are a by-product of such correspondence have little aesthetic appeal when wrenched out of this context and viewed by those not engaged in the activity. Many of those involved in the *Fluxshoe*, such as Genesis P-Orridge, were also active Mail Artists. It is perfectly feasible to treat the *Fluxshoe* as an early public manifestation of Mail Art, since many of the pieces associated with it are typical of the items produced within the Eternal Network, where the constraints of postal charges lead to a concentration on paper based works and small assemblages. The stickers P-Orridge so painstakingly attached to pebbles on Hastings beach during the *Fluxshoe* are utterly representative of the items produced by Mail Artists. Likewise, Networkers often send each other scripts similar to those enacted during the Fluxshoe, then mail back and forth photographic and other records of the events they've staged. In many cases the documentation appears to be more important than the activity itself.

However, while process based, neither Fluxus nor Mail Art could operate without a specific content since pure communication would not be very interesting even if it was possible. Nevertheless, the messages being propagated by these movements are not always easy to decipher. Fluxus is dualistic in nature, on the one hand it wishes to be iconoclastic and modernising, on the other it draws upon occult traditions that may or may not have been handed down from antiquity. Fluxus took up both the Dadaist gag and Surrealist mysticism. Maciunas claimed he wanted to 'purge the world of Europeanism', while simultaneously indulging in a great deal of pseudo-Latinisation, which began with the name Fluxus and has been continued right the way through to the title of this talk.

Even if the nostalgic use of Latin was merely a way of making Fluxus innovations look even more new fangled and up to the minute, by providing them with an antiquated counterpoint, the technique that was employed to create this tension between two very differently charged poles has been known to occultists since at least the time of the renaissance.[1] This bifurcation between modernising and nostalgic impulses which is a characteristic of Fluxus as a movement, is more readily apparent in Maciunas as an individual than any other member of the group. Certainly, after Henry Flynt, Maciunas was the most iconoclastic of the Fluxus circle, and he out-did everyone else in his insistence on gags and humour. Likewise, as the man who packaged Fluxus for public consumption, Maciunas did more than anyone else to make the movement appear like a nostalgic re-enactment of the Dadaist revolt.[2] While Maciunas was an adept of Retro-Futurism, there can be no doubt about the fact that Joseph Beuys was more deeply committed to shamanism than any other member of the Fluxus group.

Beuys was a disciple of Rudolf Steiner, who understood the evolution of the earth as being the result of a constant cooling down and hardening of spirit into matter. At the top of the spiritual sphere is the divine and at the other end of the scale we find stones. While spirit is present in every being, there is a danger that the things in the middle, such as men and wimmin, will turn into stone. A spiritual leader is required to reverse this process and Beuys saw the modern artist as filling this role. This is why in his sculptural work, Beuys uses fat which is fluid when warm and hard when it's cold. This element was employed in combination with felt, an insulating material made from animal hair. Therefore, when Beuys attached a strip of felt to a pile of fat, it was an act of shamanism, an attempt to spiritualise matter.

Fluxus makes a great deal of sense when read in the light of occult theories, since the group shared with the Situationists a concern with poeticising the everyday. The constant transformation of ordinary objects and events into art, and art into the everyday, is a modern form of alchemy. Such an understanding explains the iconic power of a number of assemblages created for the *Fluxshoe* which bring together objects as diverse as a magnet, a lemon and a thimble. Likewise, Genesis P-Orridge, who participated in the *Fluxshoe*, has a particularly deep fascination with bodily fluids. He is notorious for an exhibition at the ICA in 1976 that featured used tampons.[3] However, this work clearly has more depth than has been accorded to it by those who view the piece as a simple shock statement. The occult significance of menstrual blood is obvious enough and again, as in the work of Beuys, we are being presented with a substance that was once fluid but has subsequently congealed.

In the early eighties, P-Orridge and David Tibet formed the Temple ov Psychic Youth, a very loosely structured occult order that set out to free the magickal tradition of its archaic entanglements and fuse it with a practical concern for improving everyday life. In order to understand the tradition of which Fluxus forms a part, it is necessary to appreciate that the avant-garde largely operates outside the institution of art, and although P-Orridge no longer has anything to do with TOPY, there is a direct line of transmission through his Mail Art activities to the Temple, making this organisation far closer to what Maciunas envisioned as the outcome of Retro-Futurist activities than the aesthetic garbage being perpetrated by those artists who are now claiming affiliations with Fluxus for careerist purposes.

A classic example of this bandwagon jumping was the *Violence of the Imagination* event that took place at the Zap Club, Brighton in February 1994. The careerists who organised this charade invoked the historical avant-garde in the form of Futurism, Dadaism, Fluxus, Neoism and the Situationists but demonstrated their complete ignorance of all theoretical issues at the panel talks that closed the 'festival'. Those responsible for this sham were consistently apologetic about their use of the word violence (which was unsuccessfully used as a come on in an attempt to get the public to part with its cash) and justified it in terms of 'healing psychological wounds' caused by aggression! They had no understanding of violence as a productive element contributing to social transformation or the problems of definition associated with the word, the ruling class having consistently used this as a pejorative term for the activities of their opponents while wrapping their own use of force in a cloak of legality. It has, of course, been a cliché since the time of Bakunin that 'the urge to destroy is also a creative urge'. However, both this and the notion that the critique of the institution of art is fundamental to the avant-garde, proved too difficult for these dilettantes to get into their thick skulls.[4]

Moving back to genuine avant-garde movements and away from cheap careerist fakes, another contemporary group deeply concerned with the occult is the London Psychogeographical Association. The LPA emerged from the Situationist current within the avant-garde and has skilfully fused the praxis of the Debordist and Nashist elements of that bifurcated 'movement'. Scandinavian Situationism is relatively unknown in Anglo-American circles but it is a good deal closer to the activities of Fluxus than its more familiar French counterpart. The LPA are particularly concerned with the way in which the establishment uses ritual and ley-lines to gain a stranglehold over everyday life. However, some of the LPA's less historically grounded activities throw into sharp relief the similarities and differences between Fluxus and the Situationists. Taking their cue from Asger Jorn's suggestion in his 1966 book *The Order Of Nature*, the LPA has organised a number of three sided football matches. Three teams play with a single ball, each defending their own goal with a record being kept of the goals each concedes. The flow of the game is enlivened by strategic and practical decisions, as well as diplomacy. Whereas Fluxus soccer played with two teams and two balls results in a faster and less focused game, the LPA variant raises the possibility of alliances as well as rivalry.

Even closer to Fluxus than the LPA is the Neoist group, who have been described by Henry Flynt as an off-shoot of the movement founded by Maciunas. Neoism emerged from the Mail Art Network in the late seventies. The Neoists shared the preoccupation of the Fluxus group with short scripted performances, games, gags and bizarre assemblages produced under the influence of occult philosophy. Likewise, a large part of the group's iconography harked back to Futurism and Dada. If one were to pick a single object to represent Dadaism, an obvious choice would be the iron with tacks attached to subvert its intended use. In creating the central icon of their movement, the Neoists appropriated this idea but also improved upon it. At their performances, the Neoists would take ordinary steam irons and paint highly inflammable glues onto the smooth surface intended for creasing clothes, then set light to the adhesive. These flaming steam irons were subversive in exactly the same way as the Dadaist icon from which the Neoists had drawn inspiration, but the effect was simultaneously more spectacular and less threatening. Likewise, the burning iron was extremely close to Fluxus in the way it used an occult element to invoke the ephemeral nature of the circus and vaudeville.

Another movement to emerge from the Mail Art network was the Church of the SubGenius, a parody of fundamentalist religion whose adherents worshipped a salesman called J. R. 'Bob' Dobbs, a pretty regular guy who just happened to be endowed with supernatural powers and enormous wealth. The SubGenius shared the Maciunas obsession with gags and vaudeville, but beneath their scornful parody of fundamentalist Christianity, there was a longing for fusion with a mystical force, in the form of UFO cults and heretical millenniumism. Perhaps Ivan Stang, who founded the cult, should have applied Sorel's comments on the genesis of political ideologies to the field of religion. In his book *The Illusions Of Progress*, the French thinker observed that: 'Every scholastic formulation of political principles will have the same destiny; after having amused the literati, it will end up furnishing justification to groups whose existence the author had not even suspected'. Even if the majority of SubGenii haven't yet embraced a post-industrial fundamentalism, there are certainly fundamentalists who cite the Church of the SubGenius as a practising Satanist cult.

It is impossible to say how many movements of this type are active at the moment, there are certainly hundreds if not thousands. In Glasgow alone, which is a very small city, I know of three groups that are active in the tradition that encompasses Fluxus and the Situationists. The Dadanarchists, whose name ought to be enough to explain what they are about, are very close to the spirit of Fluxus. The Archaeogeodetic Association are chiefly concerned with the interrelationship between psychogeography, ley-lines and astrology; while the Workshop for a Non-Linear Architecture obsessively drift about the city seeking out the unconscious solicitations of the urban environment in the manner of the Surrealists, Lettristes and Situationists.

I want to conclude by explaining why it is healthy that there should be a Fluxus exhibition at the Tate. This comes down to a question of practicality, major museums are in a position to provide public access to information about avant-garde movements that are no longer active. Exhibitions such as *Fluxbritannica*, which draws very heavily on the *Fluxshoe* archive, can provide inspiration for a new generation of activists who will develop their praxis with greater efficacy if data about the historical avant-garde is readily available. Fluxus and the Situationists are now a part of cultural history. Neoism is dead and its inevitable recognition as a precursor to the more substantial Plagiarist and Art Strike movements is simply a matter of time. As I've outlined, new movements are now tilling the soil once tended by groups such as the Futurists and Dadaists, while events like *Violence of the Imagination* are pathetic attempts to cash-in on the belated recognition accorded to genuine innovators. Beware of cheap imitations and unproductive falsifications of history.

Notes for a lecture at the Tate Gallery 28/4/94.

1 While occultists spend a great deal of time faking the antiquity of the activities in which they are engaged, the avant-garde's insistence on the element of innovation within its creations leads to a spurious denial of its historic roots. In this sense, the avant-garde and the occult are two sides of the same coin, they are the positive and negative poles which generate that multifarious enigma known as contemporary society.

2 As Marx notes in *The Eighteenth Brumaire Of Louis Bonaparte*: 'Men make their own history, but not of their own free will... just when they appear to be engaged in a revolutionary transformation of themselves and their material surroundings, in the creation of something that does not yet exist... they timidly conjure up the spirits of the past to help them; they borrow their names, slogans and costumes so as to stage the new world-historical scene in this venerable disguise and borrowed language.'

3 This work, alongside much else that P-Orridge did in the seventies, such as his participation in the *Fluxshoe*, was done in collaboration with Cosey Fanny Tutti. Unfortunately, lack of space prevents me from detailing this in depth, or including information on Tutti's activity as a 'nude model' cum 'performance artist'. Since Tutti was not involved with TOPY, I did not invoke her name in this talk.

4 These two panel talks were chaired by a womun who usually facilitates business conferences and who knew absolutely nothing about the avant-garde. This could have led to a situation that paralleled the SI conference at the ICA in 1960 or the lectures Devi Det Hompson gave during the *Fluxshoe* with a gag tied securely around his mouth. However, the presence of 'artists' such as Boris Nieslony and Monica Ross prevented anything interesting from happening. These two buffoons rabbited on about 'acceptance', adopting all the rhetorical tricks favoured by that 'extremist of the centre', the liberal.

Ross was hell bent on getting everyone present to accept the ruling class definition of violence by actively sabotaging any attempt to debate the dynamics of the discourse constructed around the word, her neo-hippie doctrines being patently reactionary because they amount to an ideology of social peace. Most of those present hadn't even got as far as understanding clichés about the issue that can be found in pulp novels such as *Who Killed*

Enoch Powell? by Arthur Wise (Sphere, London 1972): '...violence was the only political tool available... by which they might radically change the social situation in which they found themselves... violence was the final communicative act of a man in the last stages of what the Catholics call despair.' Since readers of mass market paperbacks effortlessly understand these things, self-styled 'artists' and 'intellectuals' ought to be able to get their heads around them. Even taking into account the presence of Ross, who had no intention of 'accepting' the opinions of anyone who questioned her reactionary views and institutional credentials, this is not asking much. However, understanding was beyond most of those present, an air of despair hung over the room as Ross whinged on and on, until at last she was forced to retract the 'universality' of her proclamations when I pointed out that without making critical judgements, one would be left 'accepting' the notions of ethnicity promoted by racists.

The Holborn Working
10 July 1994

BOLSHEVISM AND NATIONAL SOCIALISM were the twin currents that marked the final bifurcation of science and religion. They were contemporaries, although only in a relatively conscious manner, of the last ditch defence of the Newtonian world-view and the ultimate defeat of this ideology, which left them imprisoned on the same 'intellectual' field, whose degradation they announced. It is now a cliché within both liberal and libertarian circles to announce that Bolshevism and National Socialism were at once historically related and opposed. This opposition, which each considered to be their most important aspect and 'radical' contribution, revealed the internal inadequacy of their critique and its one-sided development. National Socialism wanted to suppress Masonry without realising it; Bolshevism wanted to realise Masonry without suppressing it. The critical position now elaborated by the Neoist Alliance shows that the realisation and suppression of Masonry are inseparable aspects of a single supersession of Sufi traditions in their Templar form.

Anyone who has allowed the scales to fall from their eyes can see that the world's top occultists are to be found among the ruling class and that those New Age groups who attract disciples by offering training in 'chaos magick', 'creative visualisation' or 'rubbing the Buddha for money', are worse than mere rank amateurs, they are shameless charlatans. Indeed, many of them are quite consciously working to prevent the development of a system of symbol manipulation that is completely autonomous of the state. Currently, Masonry is marshalled in defence of the status quo, but as the Bavarian Illuminati demonstrated in the eighteenth-century, power always flows in two directions and it rarely emanates from what is widely misperceived as constituting the 'centre'. The cellular form of secret societies devised by the founders for the security of the movement, can as readily be used to hoodwink the leadership, who thus become unwitting front men for activities they would never countenance. By infiltrating the Lodges of Masonry, it is possible to spread a heretical message of freedom across the world.

Nevertheless, there is a dual movement to all our activities and the dawn ritual conducted outside the Grand Lodge in London served to reduce the power of conservative elements within the Craft by applying the energies accumulated around their headquarters to progressive ends. The building itself, on Great Queen Street, mid-way between Holborn and Covent Garden tube stations, is imposing but generally featureless. From a distance the Grand Lodge, with its 200 foot tower, appears impressive. Close up it is rather dull, consisting as it does of flat stone work with very few decorative motifs. The eastern flank of the Grand Lodge incorporates a bank and various shops, while part of the northern side is given over to the Connaught Rooms, a Masonic bar and restaurant. Thus the casual observer is left with the impression that the Grand Lodge is not an individual unit but forms part of a block – and, as every Fleet Street hack knows, it's possible for 'regular' Masons to enter the building directly from the Connaught Rooms, thus avoiding the embarrassment of being exposed as 'on the square' among 'the profane'. As befits a secret society, Masonry's detachment from the rest of the world is not visible from the outside. A gap separates everything but the entrance to the Grand Temple from the rest of the building, which encloses it. Other than this, the United Grand Lodge is taken up with offices, meeting rooms, small temples, reception rooms, a library and a museum. Running on a bi-monthly schedule, a variety of these chambers are rented out to London's innumerable 'regular' Lodges.

However, rather than presenting further observations of my own about the building, which would offer the attentive reader a good many clues to the substance of the Holborn working – obviously such things are only revealed to initiates of the Neoist Alliance – we shall instead quote Harold P. Clunn's description of the site, from his book *The Face Of London*: 'The last remnant of squalor and poverty has now been removed from… Kingsway by the erection of the fine Masonic Temple, built at a cost of £1, 000, 000. It was opened by the Duke of Connaught on 19 July 1933, who also laid the foundation-stone on 14 July 1927. It covers a huge triangular site, previously occupied by some of the worst slums in London… the Masonic Temple… presents a vista of almost Eastern splendour when seen from Long Acre. A sort of square has been formed at the western end of

Great Queen Street by... extensive road-widening opposite the Masonic Temple and Wild Street.'

To move on to less immediately visible matters, while our occult theology is not unrelated to the assemblage of symbols found within Royal Arch Masonry, it clearly has a far greater historical import than a belief system built upon Pagan nostalgia. Just as the French Revolution was conducted in the costumes of ancient Rome, so its Freemasonic patrons abandoned Christ in their revival of Jehovah, Lucifer and Osiris – this choice of idols reflects the excessive love of the classical and pre-classical world prevalent among educated minds during that period of European history. Obviously, the theological innovations of The Process Church Of The Final Judgement – which shifted the devotional habits of post-Masonic thinkers towards Jehovah, Lucifer and Christ – constituted a considerable advance upon Royal Arch teachings. However, only the Neoist Alliance trinity of Marx, Christ and Satan united in struggle, accurately embodies the religious world view of the coming centuries.

Since the avant-garde of this century is a highly advanced outgrowth of post-Masonic culture, it has never sought recognition from the deeply conservative United Grand Lodge. Nevertheless, the covert connections between so called 'anti-art' and the Brotherhood are on open display to anyone with the ability to read the relevant signs. Dadaism was launched under the aegis of a club called the Cabaret Voltaire. As both a Mason, and one of the chief architects of the French revolution, Voltaire's name has often been used in the titles of Lodges affiliated to continental Grand Orient Masonry. Similarly, the fact that two leading members of the Lettriste Movement, Isidore Isou and Maurice Lemaitre, were introduced to each other by Louis Pauwels – co-author of the notorious *Morning of the Magicians* – is a matter of public knowledge. Likewise, Isou's adopted name can be read etymologically as Jesus Jesus, while Lettrisme itself is actually an advanced form of Qabalah whose real purpose is hidden from the profane under the guise of an 'art' movement.

A fast rising star of early Lettrisme, Ivan Chtcheglov, wrote the founding document of another Masonic organisation, the Situationist International. *Formulary For A New Urbanism* is a bold statement that makes typically ambiguous use of Masonic coded language in both its title and the main body of the text, by these means Chtcheglov laid the foundations for the Situationist's esoteric use of architectural and geographical imagery. The work begins with the observation that 'there is no longer any Temple of the Sun'. The Lettristes, and later the Situationists, were deeply disturbed by the fact that within 33rd degree Masonry the final syllable of the secret word JAHBULON was widely understood to refer to the Biblical city of On – more recently Heliopolis – during the period in which the monumental architecture erected to honour Ra, the Sun God, was re-dedicated to Osiris, the God of the Dead. As far as these post-war Parisian Qabalists were concerned, most Masons were making a fundamental theological error in taking their Light solely from Lucifer – referred to as Baal but corrupted to BUL within the secret word for God. Both the Lettristes and the Situationists felt that ON symbolised a broad period of Egyptian history and thus a sense of balance between darkness and light. The Neoist Alliance considers the Situationist obsession with harmony – usually expressed negatively through the use of what profane eyes misread as 'political' terminology clustered around the concept of 'reification' – to be one-sided. However, this does not blind us to the beautifully poetic way in which the SI developed the deeply coded form of Qabalah that Marx learnt from Hegel. Returning briefly to Chtcheglov, he later revealed that the 'secret chiefs' who controlled the Situationist International were based in Tibet, as had also been the case with a British forerunner of the group, the Hermetic Order of the Golden Dawn..

From the above, it will be obvious to the attentive reader that the simultaneous realisation and suppression of Masonry will establish convincingly that in the many different – and necessarily mutually exclusive wills of wo/mankind – there is a common will that cannot be renounced. Since the notion of the 'total man' has been decisively exposed as an aristocratic fraud, our individual concerns are undoubtedly our only salvation. Three cheers for the Egoist who thinks only of herself! Once Masonry is realised and suppressed, social disintegration will be re-established at a higher level. From this time forth, religion in realising itself, will celebrate in feast its inability to reconcile darkness and light. The spontaneous appearance of division in unity and unity in division, make it unnecessary for the Lion to lie down with the Lamb. Humanity is the Devil, mean and corrupt, a liar blinded by her own deceptions – and so out will come the tricolour cockades and ribbons, decorating everything that is without consequence. Religion will separate itself from beauty too! Jacques de Molay, thou art avenged.

Neoism, Plagiarism and Praxis

A document presented to individuals who have been invited to join the Neoist Alliance. On the basis of a number of texts of this type, Candidates for the Order are expected to make a carefully considered decision about whether or not they wish to be initiated into one of our Chapels. Candidates are then tested on this material before being allowed to proceed further into an understanding of our mysteries.

Carlos

CARLOS THE JACKAL HAS BEEN CAGED, the western media rejoices and in this celebratory fashion, the press has ushered in a new era of paranoia. The Venezuelan belongs to the old school who specialised in hi-jackings and assassinations. In his middle-age, Carlos is an anachronism and western spooks are now using this media icon to remind those who nominally employ them that their services are indispensable if the world is to be 'made safe for democracy'. It is highly convenient that, as the London *Sunday Times* so eloquently put it, 'no sooner had the world rejoiced at the capture of Ilich Ramirez Sanchez, the celebrity terrorist of the 1970s, than a new menace emerged: a nuclear market for backroom bomb makers.' In other words, at the very moment nineteen-seventies style 'revolutionary' mayhem is finally neutralised, the 'threat' of nuclear terrorism is to be exploited by the many journalists who work for the intelligence services to the mutual benefit of themselves and their paymasters.

Given this state of affairs, it's hardly surprising that the press has presented Carlos to its readers as being simultaneously villainous and comic, recasting his life as the tragic story of how a bumbling psychopath became known as the most dangerous man in the world. One of the more sordid aspects of the Jackal's arrest was its exploitation as an opportunity for under-the-line advertising of Johnny Walker whiskey. The media necessarily played a key role in these illicit promotions, with the fact that Carlos had a penchant for this brand of scotch being mentioned in many of the news reports about his capture. If the Jackal had been a 100 Pipers man, I might have a little more respect for him, but thanks in no small part to his consumption of Johnny Walker Red Label, Carlos comes across like a failed method actor angling for the lead role in a B movie about an ageing drug baron being edged out of business by younger and more vicious hoodlums. The Jackal possesses all the trappings of a sad old bastard, from the tendency to reminisce about his 'glory days' right the way through to a hernia and a girlfriend twenty years younger than himself

While much of the media is busy portraying Carlos as evil, his small but vocal fan club within anarchist and left-wing circles persist in simplistically praising their hero's bold 'revolutionary' acts. Rather like the groupies who stalk the inmates of America's death row, innumerable Carlos freaks believe they are transgressing dominant values when all they are really doing is creating a mirror image of the world as it is. Topsy-turvy thinking of this type was long ago taken to its logical conclusion by an American neo-Nazi group called the Universal Order, who view Charles Manson as their 'Fuhrer'. However, there are more sophisticated responses to the activities of the Jackal and his associates. In its more populist guise, one of these can be summarised under the heading 'Terrorism Is Theatre', which is used as the title of the opening chapter of a book called *The Carlos Complex* by British journalists Christopher Dobson and Ronald Payne.

If, as Dobson and Payne suggest, 'terrorism' is 'planned for public effect, not for military targets' and has no real strategic aims, then rather than resembling 'theatre', its 'irrationality' is closer to the techniques employed by avant-garde movements such as Futurism, Dada and Fluxus. Indeed, the parallels are remarkable, not only is there the same focus on breaking down traditional narrative structures and instead emphasising individual and apparently isolated events, both 'Terror International' and the avant-garde consist of several tightly knit and overlapping groups operating under a variety of organisational names. Just as it is difficult to explain the activities of Carlos to the uninitiated without mentioning the Baader-Meinhof Gang or the Japanese Red Army, so when summarising the achievements of the Fluxus group, intelligent discussion requires reference to contemporary rivals and collaborators such as Auto-Destructive Art, Gutai, Actual, the Situationists and the Happenings movement.

The supposition that there is a link between the avant-garde and the activities of urban guerrillas has become something of a cliché in the Anglo-American media over recent years. The more upmarket sections of the press have run endless features about 'art terrorism', which generally consist of little more than anecdotes about media pranks pulled by individuals working in what can loosely be described as the cultural tradition derived from Futurism and Dada.

It is therefore inevitable that fringe intellectuals will begin to consume the media spectacles orchestrated by the various groups associated with Carlos as works of performance art. Since the individuals being drawn into this discourse are well versed in the theoretical basis of avant-gardism, its course of development is utterly predictable. Carlos himself is suspect, over-exposure in the press and the recent 'capture' have completely eroded his mystique. The chief theorist of Fluxus, George Maciunas, drew a distinction between 'the monomorphic neo-haiku flux event' and 'the mixed media neo-baroque happening'; the career of the Jackal smacks suspiciously of the latter.

When divorced from its political context and viewed through the perspective of avant-garde aesthetics, the Lod airport massacre performed by the Japanese Red Army in May 1972 is without doubt the most sublime act of 'Terror International'. Three members of the JRA troupe who'd just arrived in Israel from Rome walked into the arrival lounge, removed submachine guns from their hand luggage and sprayed their fellow passengers with hot lead. Twenty-six people died and another eighty were wounded before two of the actors were killed and the third captured.

André Breton had long ago insisted that the ultimate Surrealist act consisted of randomly firing a revolver into a crowd. The Lod airport 'happening' was simply the realisation of this dictum through the use of modern weaponry. However, it would be wrong to conclude from this that the JRA is not rooted in the past or that it entirely escaped the conventions of the particular culture from which it emerged. Like all avant-gardists, 'Terror International' established its 'modernity' through the double-bind of incorporating archaic elements into its activities. In the case of the JRA, the troupe's fame dates from the March 1970 hi-jack of a Japanese airliner using Samurai swords instead of more contemporary weapons such as guns. It is the tension established between this embrace of tradition and the use of genuine innovations which creates the illusion that the avant-garde is at the cutting edge of social change.

While all the groups clustered around Carlos and the PFLP were absorbed by the cult of violence, the JRA were particularly mystical in their disregard for life, believing that death during the course of their 'revolutionary' happenings would result in union with the three stars of Orion. The use by 'Terror International' of this combination of myth and violence is reminiscent of the theoretical outlook of Georges Sorel, the scourge of social decadence and prophet of the general strike, whose writings were a huge influence on Marinetti and the Futurist movement. This conjunction of perspectives serves to illustrate one of the many ways in which the activities of Carlos and his associates could be absorbed into the history and practice of performance art.

Equally, the words of Group Zero's Otto Piene can be interpreted as a call to arms: 'We, the artists, with serious concerns, have to face reality, wake up, move out of the art world and embrace the void'. Likewise, the influence of the Situationist International on the Angry Brigade, an English urban guerrilla group of the early seventies, is well documented and this troupe's use of terminology such as 'spectacle' in communiqués enabled the police to identify them as 'anarchist' inspired. However, there are innumerable other ways of understanding the significance of 'terrorism', many of which produce results that are considerably more sublime than those obtained from pure aesthetics.

The Carlos 'legend' is still being milked by western propagandists, the Jackal's stint as a student at Patrice Lumumba University in Moscow being considered more than sufficient proof that he was a KGB agent. However, nothing in the world of spookery is straight forward and since his activities greatly benefited the CIA/MI6, it is just as likely that Carlos was working for the British and Americans. This scenario isn't nearly as bizarre as it may at first appear, thanks to the cell structure of para-military organisations, individuals joining groups of this type have no idea who is directing their actions.

Becoming an urban guerrilla has remarkable parallels with joining the Freemasons, it is a commitment made in blind faith, as the example of Italy demonstrates so well. While the majority of individuals who saw 'active service' with the Red Brigades genuinely adhered to left-wing ideals, their activities were ultimately directed by members of the security services and blended perfectly with right-wing atrocities such as the Bologna Station massacre, that had initially been blamed on communist elements. In Philip Willan's 1991 book *Puppet Masters: The Political Use of Terrorism in Italy*, the Red Brigades are described as having a three tier structure; the young fanatics, the Eastern Bloc agents and 'further in, in the most secret compartment, the infiltrators of the Interior Ministry and Western secret services'. The Red Brigades were, of course, part of the PFLP inner circle in Europe and while these and other groups claimed to be 'marxist revolutionaries', the fact that their activities were of such obvious benefit to the security services in both cold war camps, results in assertions of this type appearing suspicious.

Personally, I do not subscribe to conspiracy theories that suggest the destiny of the world is controlled by a cabal of thirteen men who meet in a darkened room. Obviously, various forces are competing for dominance within the world, and even the more successful of these ruling elites are riven by factionalism and rivalry. The success of the Anglo-American 'security' system established in the aftermath of the Second World War rested, at least partially, upon the fact that it remained unseen by the mass of those whose lives were circumscribed by it. While the role the British and Americans played in the establishment of the post-war intelligence services throughout Europe is most readily evident in Italy, their influence certainly wasn't confined to this single defeated Axis power. Likewise, there can be little doubt that this state of affairs gave London and particularly Washington, great power and political leverage across the whole of Western Europe.

In the latest issue of the maverick London based journal *Perspectives,* someone calling himself Peter Drew makes a number of observations about the security services and writes explicitly about a CIA inspired scheme code named Gladio which has received considerable coverage in the British 'quality' press in recent years. After repeating what was already widely known about the plan to use anti-communist far-right groups as a disownable guerrilla army against the cold war foe, Drew then says it 'is now believed that some of these, particularly in Germany, are being used to foment political and xenophobic violence and destabilise the USA's new enemy – a united Europe'. Drew also makes reference to the fact that Robin Ramsey, editor of the left-wing and generally reliable conspiracy journal *Lobster*, recently reprinted the one statement cut from an early eighties television programme on British intelligence. It was made by a former BOSS agent Gordon Winter and ran as follows: 'British intelligence has a saying that if there is a left-wing movement in Britain bigger than a football team our man is the captain or the vice captain, and if not, he is the referee and he can send any man off the field and call our man on at any time he likes.'

Now, if British intelligence is in the habit of providing leadership to 'subversive elements' within the United Kingdom, it would make sense for the CIA to control from above the activities of its foreign 'enemies'. I am not suggesting that control of Carlos and his Commando Boudia, or interlocking groups such as the JRA, was necessarily as direct as that exerted on the Italian Red Brigades. However, since it was the Anglo-American security establishment who reaped the major propaganda benefits from the media 'happenings' of 'Terror International', it would not be surprising to discover that they pulled at least some of the strings animating the PFLP puppet.

It was in the spooks interest to perpetuate the cold war and they quickly created a minor cultural industry in the form of books and articles linking 'international terrorism' to Moscow. That they were well placed to maximise the propaganda potential of 'terrorism' is made readily evident by works such as Stephen Dorril's *The Silent Conspiracy: Inside the Intelligence Services in the 1990s*: 'Journalism has been a natural recruiting ground for the security services. John le Carré, who worked for M16 between 1960 and 1964, has made the astonishing statement that "the British Secret Service controlled large sections of the press, just as they may do today". In 1975, following Senate hearings on the CIA which had revealed the extent of agency recruitment of both American and British journalists, sources let it be known that half the foreign staff of a British daily were on the MI6 payroll. In the mid-eighties, the present author was given, by a senior *Observer* journalist, a list of five foreign affairs journalists on a Sunday newspaper who had acted as correspondents for the intelligent services. No doubt the practice continues to this day.' Certainly, as recently as this month, the British journalist Patrick Seale felt it necessary to issue a statement denying that he ran MI6's Beirut bureau when he was the *Observer's* Middle East correspondent.

However, intelligence influence in the publishing industry extents well beyond the employment of journalists to gather data and spread disinformation through the press. A *Sunday Times* feature of 19/9/93 by Nigel West entitled 'Literary Agents', revealed that a good many novelists, particularly those working in the thriller genre, were security service employees. This article appeared to be partially inspired by a more detailed account of the phenomena given in a 1987 book by Anthony Masters called *Literary Agents: The Novelist as Spy*. Many spy thrillers are little more than Anglo-American intelligence propaganda, and a pertinent example is the 1976 publication *Carlos Terror International* by Dennis Eisenberg and Eli Landau, promoted with the blurb: 'the novel that is closer to the truth than anyone dares to believe...' The book name checks urban guerrilla groups from across the world: 'As for West Germany, there have been indications that the Baader-Meinhof murder-gang are again gaining in strength'. The inevitable conclusion is the 'same we would reach if we had an interest in weakening the West and fostering anarchy – unite all these factors under one umbrella – an umbrella known as Terror International'.

However, whether or not it was directly controlled by the CIA, 'Terror International' was more than simply a vehicle for cold war propaganda which sought to justify increased surveillance and other repressive measures in the western 'democracies', while simultaneously helping to secure those all important increases in 'defence' and espionage budgets. The Jackal's greatest personal triumph was the raid on the OPEC headquarters in Vienna in December 1975. Once the building had been stormed, the hostages were divided into four categories; Friends, Enemies, Neutrals and Austrians. The 'Friends' were the Libyans, Algerians, Iraqis and Kuwaitis. The enemies were the officials representing Saudi Arabia, Iran, Abu Dhabi and Qatar. In this way, the activities of 'Terror International' were perfectly suited to protecting the interests of the Anglo-American establishment. The PFLP and their inner circle in Europe were a not unimportant factor in reinforcing those divisions that already existed between a number of middle eastern states. In this way, Carlos and his associates assisted in minimising the chances of OPEC functioning as an effective oil cartel.

I do not wish to suggest that the PFLP was simply an arm of the CIA. Certainly, many of the politically naive urban guerrillas who saw active service with 'Terror International' initially committed themselves to para-military tactics because they adhered to a political programme that was at complete variance with the aims and interests of the Anglo-American establishment. At certain times, these 'revolutionaries' may even have been able to act in accord with their 'marxist' principles. However, the clandestine nature of the organisations to which they belonged provided ample opportunity for manipulation by both Washington and Moscow. If 'Terror International' was a political football, it's logical to conclude that the Anglo-American establishment supplied the referee, because this side scored the vast majority of goals during the course of a long and toughly contested game. Since we now know that the CIA was able to exercise at least some control over the Red Brigades, there is a distinct possibility that they succeeded in directing the activities of the other urban guerrilla organisations co-ordinated by Carlos.

Dobson and Payne are therefore wrong to suggest that the activities of

'Terror International' had no real strategic aims. From the perspective of the Anglo-American establishment, they were a perfect covert compliment to official policy. In middle-age, Carlos isn't much use to anyone as an urban guerrilla. Now is a particularly convenient time to haul him before the courts and thereby demonstrate that the western 'democracies' are still vigilantly guarding themselves against the many 'enemies' who threaten their very existence. And the successful persecution of a spent force immediately after the Aldrich Ames spy-scandal can't do any harm. In their different ways, these two events provide justification for spiralling intelligence budgets in our increasingly insecure world.

To nobody's surprise, the Anglo-American establishment continues to perfect its own unique technology of repression, with vast amounts of money being poured into the development of frequency weapons and methods of electronic control. In the final analysis, it doesn't matter who Carlos worked for or what motivated his activities, he served the cause of reaction by playing the role of an urban guerrilla on a pitch marked out by the Anglo-American establishment and according to the rules they'd instituted for the 'strategy of tension' game. Little that is good is likely to emerge from the capture of the Jackal. The most we can hope for is the rehabilitation of that classic fashion item, the white trenchcoat, as worn by Carlos during the OPEC raid of December 1975. As a celebrity 'terrorist', the Jackal is the perfect hook on which to sell ideologies, whiskey and clothes.

First published by the German magazine *Konkret*, October 1994

Sixty years of treason

IT HAS BEEN OBSERVED ELSEWHERE that for the development of every language, the acceptance of foreign elements is essential. No people lives for itself. Every enduring intercourse with other peoples results in the borrowing of words from their language, this is quite indispensable to reciprocal cultural fecundation. The countless points of contact which culture daily creates between people leave their traces in language. New objects, ideas, concepts – religious, political and generally social – lead to new expressions and word formations. But this is precisely what is lacking in so called 'high' culture in this country.

German philosophy became significant when Kant simultaneously united and superseded the rival discourses established by Leibniz on the one hand, and that trajectory represented by Hobbes and Hume on the other. British philosophy has been degenerating for the past sixty years, and the same is true of every aspect of official English 'culture'. Transferring one's attention from the New Learning of Francis Bacon, to the so called 'New Poetry' of today, is to go from the sublime to the ridiculous. The former is the creation of a rising class in the first flush of youthful vigour, while the latter is the senseless babbling of senility.

The poet, as represented by the likes of Graig Raine and the succeeding generation producing so called 'New Poetry', is completely egocentric, trapped inside himself, incapable of empathising or identifying with others, of love, friendship, affection or tenderness. He is a completely isolated unit, incapable of rapport with anyone. His responses are entirely visceral, not cerebral, his intelligence is a mere tool in the service of his drives and needs; he is incapable of mental passion, mental interaction, he can't relate to anything other than his own physical sensations. History, in this imbecile's mind, becomes a home-movie. He is a half-dead, unresponsive lump, incapable of giving or receiving pleasure or happiness; consequently, he is at best an utter bore, an inoffensive blob, since only those capable of absorption in others can be charming.

The official poetic culture of this country entered its final period of decline with the cowardice of Auden in the thirties. Incapable of going forwards, poetry went backwards, official poetry had no where else to go, it was dead. Auden fled to America, Spender stayed here, where as an editor of *Encounter,* he was the leading beneficiary of the underwriting of English publishing by the CIA. Along with the Cambridge spies, English poetry proves conclusively that the Oxbridge system devours intelligence and spews out shit. These are the idiots who read Milton instead of Abiezer Coppe. What they've created is a culture of mediocrity, where stupidity is rewarded and nobody has an opinion of their own. Editors are quick to sign up those writers who endlessly reproduce the bankrupt ideals of proceeding generations. Originality and individuality are to be crushed with promises of fat contracts 'if only you'd stop wasting your time and instead apply your obvious talents to the production of tasteful, inoffensive, unchallenging, literary fiction'.

Today, anyone who wants to read a book that's worthwhile, has to write it themselves. No one who fears new ideas need be afraid of the lifeless commodities thrown onto the mass market by those publishing houses active in Britain. Newspaper and magazine sales have been completely stitched up by Smiths and Menzies, they control the vast majority of the trade, their retail outlets are unimportant, it's their stranglehold on distribution that counts. Book production is no different, a few conglomerates own virtually everything. They throw one Martin Amis imitator at us after another, and hype this garbage as the future of English fiction. This is a joke, English fiction has no future. Subversive ideas would certainly sell, but don't expect to find them in your local high street, any analysis of books on terrorism and spookery quickly reveals that non-market forces set the agenda in British publishing.

Maybe you've been knocking around for a few years and the literary establishment's stone-walling of your work hasn't succeeded in getting you to shut the fuck up. No problem! A major publisher will buy you up, put out your new book and then get 'cold feet'. It's a self-fulfilling prophesy, how could the book sell if it wasn't promoted or given proper distribution? Bought up or left out in the cold, history will prove us right. Those so called 'writers' and 'editors' currently stuffing their faces at literary luncheons will be forgotten in a few years time. We know it, they know it, and this is why they're so vociferous in their attitude towards talent. The literary establishment is eaten up with tension, with frustration, at not being talented, at not being capable of pleasure of any kind, eaten up with hate – not rational hate that is directed against those who abuse, insult and enslave – but irrational, indiscriminate hate; hatred, at bottom, of their own worthlessness.

The crippled minds who support the dominant culture value decorum and good taste precisely because they are incapable of understanding 'ugliness' as anything other than a mirror image of their own deformed intellects. The literary establishment hates the sterility of the writers it promotes and so it projects this quality onto progressive cultural tendencies. However, the dominant 'culture' eventually becomes so desperate for an infusion of fresh blood that someone whose work has long been the subject of irrational hatred among the 'literati' will suddenly be invited onto the subsidised gravy train of luncheons, readings, residencies, lectureships and grants. The young dog taken up by these vampires will be bled dry in three weeks, leaving official 'culture' as sick as ever. The zombies who promote traditional literary values are incapable of facing the fact that their every last thought is a conditioned reflex, determined entirely by past experience, it's much worse than suffering from halitosis, these people have a corpse in their mouth. Our most pressing task is to bury this 'culture' of mediocrity because, like the still-born 'New Poetry', it's already dead.

Written as an introduction to a sequence of poems featured in a forthcoming Picador anthology edited by Iain Sinclair

Part 5

Appendices

Appendix One

Stewart Home interviewed by Karen Goaman and Mo Dodson

STEWART HOME HAS MADE something of a name for himself recently. He organised the Festival Of Plagiarism at Transmission Gallery in Glasgow and has previously produced work for shows such as Ruins Of Glamour/Glamour Of Ruins (Chisenhale Studios, London 1986), Desire In Ruins (Transmission Gallery, Glasgow 1987) and the Festival Of Plagiarism in London 1988 (which he co-organised with Ed Baxter and Graham Harwood). Home is one of the organisers of the Art Strike 1990-3, in which participating cultural workers will refuse all cultural activity in order to question the identity of artists and the role art plays within contemporary society.

His other interventions include editing and publishing issues of *Smile* magazine (often under the multiple name of Karen Eliot) and writing fiction (see for example the short stories *Anarchist* in *Smile* 9, London 1986, and *Class War* in *Vague* 21, London 1989). *Pure Mania*, his first novel, will be published by Polygon books later this year. The latter is in part a parody of the Richard Allen skinhead novels published by New English Library in the 1970s.

Home's first book *The Assault On Culture: Utopian Currents from Lettrisme to Class War* (Aporia Press and Unpopular Books, London 1988), traces a set of influences and traditions which can be linked to Dada and Futurism, from Lettrisme through COBRA, the Situationists, to groups such as Fluxus and Class War.

It appears that many of those who come across Home's work are intrigued, irritated, antagonised and/or repelled by it. This could be exactly the kind of reaction Home is after. This interview goes some way towards situating his work and posing some of the questions raised by it, such as the obscurity of meaning and intention, which would appear to contradict his anti-art and 'demolish serious culture' stance.

The interview is constructed from several discussions between Karen Goaman and Mo Dodson with Stewart Home.

KG: When I first came across your work, especially your writing, it seemed to be speaking to a very particular audience, you could say a clique, which I wasn't able to identify. How would you characterise your own milieu and would you say it was part of a wider movement?

SH: Well, I'd only use the term 'movement' ironically, but I would characterise the wider 'movement' with which I have some affinity as including class struggle anarchism, the direct action libertarian left. I'm often described as an anarchist by Leninists and those to the right of what, for the sake of convenience, we'll call orthodox Marxism. On the other hand, quite a lot of people in the anarchist movement don't think I'm an anarchist at all. Vernon Richards once took the trouble of putting pen to paper to tell me that what I did was meaningless to him and that he didn't consider it to be anarchy. Personally I feel more affinity with people like the journalist Tom Vague, a former punk who isn't worried about whether what he does is considered ideologically acceptable by the self-styled fuhrers of British anarchism. Basically you could describe what I'm into as anti-authoritarianism.

As for the audience for what I do, to put it crudely, it crosses over between anarchists, punks and ex-punks and avant-garde art types. A lot of people who like my fiction aren't interested in the theory or the exhibitions, and the fiction often disgusts those who might otherwise think of me as reasonably interesting and intelligent.

KG: To what extent do you think people use particular practices such as political positions and texts (for example post-modernism, Situationists, anarchism, avant-garde art, Marxism etc.) to construct an identity for themselves that differentiates them from others, as a kind of cultural or symbolic capital to mark off their own distinction?
SH: It's a factor in the use of these practices. Bourdieu provides a crisp, clearly defined, language for describing this process in his book *Distinction: a social critique of the judgement of taste*. While it's plainly ridiculous to ignore the way in which beliefs assist individuals to shape their own identities, it's equally silly to take a reductionist stand and explain all beliefs, actions and tastes, in terms of some overwhelming need to construct a sense of self. Apart from anything else, rather than freely forming our own tastes, these are partially formed for us by our class, the age we live in and numerous other factors.

KG: How have your ideas and activities developed, in terms of your own intellectual history.
SH: My education, for want of a better term, has largely been informal. When I was fourteen and first into punk, around 1976-7, I can remember reading articles in the Sunday magazines saying that punk was like Dada and Futurism. I didn't know what these things were and so over the next couple of years I gradually found out through a very unsystematic and occasional programme of reading. I'd never heard of anarchism until I saw the Sex Pistols on the *So It Goes* TV show in August '76. I thought the Pistols were fantastic so I went and looked up anarchy in a dictionary. Later on, I'd talk to people about things and they'd maybe lend me a book or suggest something I should read and I'd just follow things up myself. School and college were a waste of time, I learnt far more in my own time than I ever did through formal education. Punk was very inspiring to me as a teenager. It seemed very natural to buy a cheap electric guitar and form a band. Later on, around 1982-3, I decided that since I'd become a musician without knowing anything about music, I could become an artist without knowing anything about art.

KG: You have no formal art training?
SH: No. I did a History Of Ideas degree at Kingston Polytechnic but I was

thrown out in the final year after repeatedly criticising the way the teachers used the spectre of failure and poor grades as a means of enforcing intellectual conformity. At this time, I was interested in the whole process of legitimisation, in academia, the arts, government, and so forth. I can remember going into galleries and thinking I could make better work than the trash that was on display. But it wasn't just a question of making better work, the point was I had to go through a complex social and administrative process to get myself accepted as a 'legitimate' artist.

One of the problems connected to this process of legitimisation is that very few people have a clear definition of what art is. To me it's a subset of categories such as music, painting and writing which are arbitrarily held to be of objectively higher value than other cultural products. However, because many artists have immense difficulties understanding such a definition, my critique of art has sometimes been misunderstood as a pathological hatred of painting and sculpture.

KG: You've done an immense amount of research into the Situationists, which you've used for instance in the book *The Assault On Culture.*

SH: One of the reasons I wrote *The Assault On Culture* was to demystify the Situationists. When I was first involved with the anarchist scene in London I can remember people giving me Situationist texts to read but refusing to explain what they meant. If I told them I didn't understand their pamphlets, they told me I was stupid. If I really pressed them they'd say the Situationists provided the total revolutionary critique. To me this attitude didn't seem any different to how the teachers had behaved at school. I was in a class which was supposed to be the cream of this crappy secondary school and we were told we were too thick to read Shakespeare. So my attitude was always, well fuck you, I'll read it and keep re-reading it until I understand it just to prove you're wrong, and afterwards I'll tell you it's shit.

KG: And that motivated your research and your writing *The Assault On Culture?*

SH: Partially, I wanted the book to be a kind of bluff-your-way guide, to deprive these ex-public school boys within the anarchist movement of their specialist knowledge. But to go back to the Situationists, when I looked into the group I found that most of their ideas could be traced back to other sources such as Dada, COBRA, Marx, the Frankfurt School, Henri Lefebvre, Lukacs and so on. The Situationists just dressed this stuff up in surrealist clichés.

KG: But couldn't you say that Situationist texts were an initial conduit of some particular insights, particularly in terms of their critique of society, and that you've absorbed these insights and been more influenced by them than your very critical position would suggest?

SH: I wouldn't say that being critical of something doesn't mean you haven't been influenced by it. Influence can be negative as well as positive. But even if the Situationists had been the greatest single influence on my intellectual development and had provided posterity with the total revolutionary critique, I would still find it tactically necessary to criticise them. The point is I have to deal with individuals who use so called Situationist ideas and the myth created around the group in a very oppressive way. I've found that the most effective tactic to use against these people is to undercut the credibility of Debord and Vaneigem, both of whom were in any case poor theorists. Their rhetorical technique was basically to make gross generalisations but state them as though they were incontrovertible fact. The idea seems to have been to convert other people – primarily students – to Situationist beliefs and practices. As part and parcel of this process, the reader was encouraged to treat this propaganda as theory. As a result it's very difficult to get individuals who've undergone a political conversion from devouring these texts to view them critically.

KG: But what you've said about Situationist texts seems to apply to your own writing, for instance in *Smile*.
SH: Yeah, but the texts in *Smile* are parodies of Situationist writing.

KG: But people don't always understand your use of irony. A rather notorious example is your paragraph on Ecological Politics in *Smile* No. 9. You write, for example, 'There is no other ideology as reactionary as ecology, as the idea that we shouldn't wipe rain forests from the earth's terrain, that we shouldn't build nuclear reactors.'
SH: That was satire, a parody of the kind of sweeping generalisations made in Situationist texts. There were some pro-Situationists who took it at face value and thought it was great. Then they met one of my friends and were ranting on at him about creating a Situationist revolution and for some reason they quoted the piece on ecology from *Smile* and my friend said 'Oh, you should meet Stewart, he's a vegetarian.' The pro-Situs got really upset, I wish I'd seen their faces as it dawned on them that not everyone else is as narrow minded as they are. If you really believe in something you should be able to articulate a reasonable argument against it, if someone can only imagine taking a single line on an issue then to me that indicates they're only dealing with it on an emotional level and haven't come to grips with the subject intellectually.

MD: But if you're using irony in a way that isn't clear, aren't you taking a very high art relationship to your audience, in the sense that, in your work, the meaning is obscure and difficult, and there are complex levels that a lot of people don't understand. You seem to be claiming a post-modernist/post-structuralist kind of relationship to your audience, in the sense that you justify irony that doesn't work by saying that your work's not closed off, it's open to multiple readings and interpretations. But with all this, you claim to be coming from a populist position, and not a high art one. This seems to me to be contradictory. It doesn't mix.
SH: A lot of popular culture is misunderstood when viewed by audiences unfamiliar with the genre to which it belongs. Bigots who want to censor gore movies don't always realise that films like the *Evil Dead* are actually slapstick comedies. Utterly ludicrous scenes, such as those showing individuals throwing themselves against walls after being possessed by evil spirits have been cited as vicious and violent by those campaigning against these films.

In the case of my writing, it takes a point and pounds it into the ground. It's deliberately relentless and very sharply focused. This would seem to mitigate against the reader assuming that meaning is being dispersed through a grid-work of adjacent discourses, which leave it open to a multiplicity of interpretations.

MD: In that sense I don't think your work is high art at all, it's very specific and non-high-art, but your justification of it tends to make it slip back into the phrasing high art people use, of there being no single meaning.

But going back to your point about popular culture, the thing is that, once you've learnt the code, the meanings aren't problematic in the same way that the text, especially for the avant-garde and 20th century high art, is always problematic.

Popular culture workers, on the other hand, are always worried about what the audience is getting. Do you ever say to yourself I want people to get my full meaning and what am I going to do about it?

SH: No, because I know from talking to people that there are already individuals who understand what I'm saying. Quite a lot of the people who don't understand what I do seem to get upset by it and that pleases me too because it seems to indicate they've realised that there's a factor involved which they haven't grasped.

MD: Supposing a lot of your audience were fascists misreading your irony and your intentions?

SH: (laughing) Well, that would tell me where their ideas were at!

MD: But to not care what your audience takes is anti-populist!

SH: I find a lot of popular culture is very cynical. In the Richard Allen skinhead books there are loads of references to the author which the audience are presumably not intended to understand. In one book there's a copper called PC Allen, in another an author called Dick Arlen. In several he has characters rave about books he'd written under other names.

MD: That's the difference between a populist who's cynical and a populist whose genuine. A cynical populist would say 'I don't want my audience to see I'm laughing up my sleeve at them, except a few of my intellectual mates'. But a genuine populist like Barbara Cartland actually believes the crap she writes – she'd be worried if people weren't feeling dewy-eyed as the hero with the ten foot jaw clasped the woman to his breast.

SH: But I don't think I need to worry about fascists liking my writing and getting what they see as a positive message from it. The way I see and depict class as a major division within society mitigates against that. Fascists see the nation as an undivided, mythic, community, so they're not going to like writing which focuses on the issue of class. It would take a very wilful misreading of my work for someone to come away from it with the impression that I have any truck with nationalism.

KG: But surely work of yours can easily be misread, take the short story *Frenzy Of The Flesh* that you put in the *Art Strike Handbook*, where you wrote about a gullible art student being sexually abused by a performance art teacher who got killed in revenge, with the art student then being murdered in a grotesquely horrible way by a homicidal anti-smoker, who was then killed by the art school technician who was the lover of the gullible art student, and who was then told he had lung cancer because he'd smoked all his life. Could somebody use it to fuel their prejudices against a particular type of bohemian person or any other oppositional type they might link to that, or could it be used to justify brutal perversion or violence? They might think...

(everybody laughing here)

SH: They might think 'This is well wicked...'

MD: What were your original intentions in that particular story?

SH: It was meant to be funny, to deflate the pretensions of a lot of performance artists and people like that. I hope it helped fuel prejudice against artists, students and bohemians. It was a piece of propaganda. I thought the best way to make the point was with humorous and very twisted moralism – anti-smoking and ultra-violence!

KG: But you don't just use violence in your fiction, for instance a lot of the videos shown during the *Festival Of Plagiarism* in Glasgow were very violent. What's your purpose in using it?

SH: Three or four of the twenty or thirty videos we screened could possibly be characterised as violent but the usage is representational – I don't really feel any need to justify it, it's not real, it's acted, it's representational.

KG: But wasn't there a real suicide on one of the videos shown at the Festival?

SH: That was taken from a live broadcast on American tv. If you're an individualist I think watching a video of a politician blowing their own brains out can be quite uplifting. I was interested in seeing how it's meaning was changed when it was used within a fictional narrative. The footage was also very heavily treated with effects, so most of the emotional impact comes from the sound.

KG: So what would you say attracts you to violence?

SH: You could say I just reflect what goes on around me. There's another argument which would explain it in terms of my identity and sense of differentiation. But that's certainly not the whole story, it's also to do with the kind of culture I've experienced ever since I went to school.

MD: So you'd entertain a kind of psychologistic interpretation or insight. That's interesting because not many 20th century artists would do that – they'd say to interpret a work as something that results from your own personal feelings of rejection, or of being bullied or needing to bully, would be an insult to their work; they'd say the work is an objective insight into a higher, a universal, reality.

SH: Well, that's bullshit! I'd say the question is not whether you're shaped by social forces but to what degree. I'm also very aware that I've a chip on my shoulder, the important thing for me is to direct my hatred against all the wankers who told me I was nothing because I went to school on a GLC overspill estate. The idea of peace and love and everybody holding hands and being mutually supportive is a complete anathema to me. However, in the case of my work the violence is, as I've said, just representation.

MD: But that's going back to the other position that you don't need to justify it – it's only representation.

SH: There's a fundamental difference

between writing about beating someone up and going out and beating someone up. Sometimes the former even appears to be more disruptive in the eyes of those in power.

MD: You could say that a liking for representations of violence is pathological.
SH: But perhaps if I didn't read or write about violence I'd behave more violently.

MD: So it's cathartic.
SH: I'm entertained by representations of violence. In my fiction I like to mix up violence and didacticism. Some people find this shocking, I think it's very funny, particularly when right-on lefties and other wankers get upset because they've missed the joke.

KG: But, to go back to a more general point about your work, in one sense it's rather post-modern, cynical and ironic, that your written work criticises or takes the piss out of the very movements (e.g.. anarchists, Situationists, Neoists etc.) which are closest to your own position, rather than attacking other movements much further removed from what you actually support – authoritarianism, political parties or whatever. On the other hand, you could argue that this kind of self-irony is an important element of anti-authoritarian practice.

The problem seems to be how people from a different position to your own might respond to this kind of self-irony, which is only understandable to a specific audience. A further problem is, to what extent can it communicate anti-authoritarian ideas outside an anti-authoritarian milieu?

I suppose I'm returning to the question I started out with, of your work appearing to be addressed to a particular clique.
SH: Well, that's because the audience, no matter how large it may be, is finite. Similarly, the people who see my work aren't some kind of abstract mass, they're specific individuals. Therefore when I'm writing something, or putting together a graphic, I think of how very specific people will respond to it. From some people I want positive responses and from others negative responses. But whatever the reaction I'm looking for, I'm trying to get a response from flesh and blood individuals. To me there's a danger that if you aim the work at what might be considered a more general audience then you'll end up addressing nobody at all. It's because what I do is intended to communicate certain very specific messages that there's an interest in it beyond the handful of people I think about when I'm actually producing it. If you're trying to communicate something then you have to be very aware of the person or people receiving your message. And I'm looking for a response, for me it has to be a two way process. I'm not interested in writing books for the sake of writing books. If there wasn't an audience for it then I wouldn't bother to produce the work.

Finally I'd disagree with you when you imply that I only attack the things that are closest to my own position. I attack, or at least highlight, authoritarianism within myself and the things that are close to me but I also criticise many individuals, groups and things, which are far removed from any anti-authoritarian milieu.

First published in *Variant* 7
Winter 1989

Appendix two

The art of Legitimation: the on-going transformation of the avant-garde from counter-cultural force to dominant institution

Stewart Home interviewed by Simon Ford

STEWART HOME'S ACTIVITIES and fields of interest have long defied categorisation. In addition to the role of prime propagandist for the Neoist Cultural Conspiracy, he is a novelist, musician, performance artist, more recently an occultist and according to at least one source, 'an ego-maniac on a world historical scale'; in short, a multifaceted avant-gardist phenomenon. After three years of high-profile inactivity (Art Strike 1990-1993), he has exploded back onto an otherwise lack-lustre cultural scene. Home's interest in the historicisation of the avant-garde ties in with my own research into the processes of legitimation. As a curator at the Victoria and Albert Museum, I have primary experience of this contentious field. Just how does a group such as Fluxus go from side-show to critical domination of a period? Museums and critics obviously have a role to play but the movements themselves are far from passive in this process. With Home's close connections to Neoism and that movement's seemingly inevitable breakthrough into what could be termed its 'historical phase', he was an obvious person to talk to about these issues.

How do you feel about the Art Strike, looking back on it now?
I'm both pleased and frustrated with the reaction to the Art Strike. One of the reasons for doing the Art Strike was to draw attention to the ways in which information about culture circulates. Rather than giving a theoretical description of how this process operates, I set up a practical demonstration of meme drift. There were odd bits of media coverage for the Strike right the way through the three years in which it took place. People were still coming across it for the first time and to them it was new and news. During the Strike, I wasn't doing any press or publicity, so information about it just bubbled up from the underground. Now that I'm doing interviews again, people want to talk to me about the Art Strike and for me, that can be boring because I want to move on. I said most of what I still had to say on the subject during the talk I gave at the Victoria and Albert Museum in January

'93. So it can be frustrating when people ask basic questions about the Strike. I'd rather not talk about the Strike unless doing so will accelerate the debate that surrounds it and my other work. I think other people deeply involved with the Strike feel this way too. Lloyd Dunn, for example, had a piece published in a US regional arts magazine called *Tractor*, summing up his thoughts on the Strike. John Berndt, tENTATIVELY a cONVENIENCE and Al Ackerman are threatening to produce documents in response to – and perhaps partially refuting – my V&A talk. This could be a foretaste of what I'd like to see happen. That is, people looking at all the material generated by the Strike and then making a serious attempt to deal with the issues raised. Actually getting hold of all the graphics and texts connected to the Art Strike is quite a task in itself because there is such a profusion of material.

The Art Strike was such an extreme thing to do. Have you ended your involvement with art completely? Or will you make any more artefacts and performances?
The Art Strike was the final wrap on all the avant-garde work I was doing during the eighties. It was the last piece of packaging placed around my post-Neoist activities before I left it to the art world to deal with my past. I'm not planning to do any further art work but I can't prevent other people interpreting my current activities as being somehow connected to the avant-garde. For example, I've set up a group called the Neoist Alliance which has nothing to do with the old Neoist Network. We've held gatherings to celebrate the founding of the Illuminati and we've picketed a Stockhausen concert in Brighton. I don't see these as art type events but I can't prevent other people from doing so. For example, the arts magazine *Hybrid* covered the demonstration against Stockhausen in its review section. I'm not complaining about that, the reviewer turned up to do a piece about a composer the Neoist Alliance detests and because we were there, ended up ignoring the music and writing about us instead. However, if you examine the coverage we got from Festival Radio and the *Brighton and Hove Leader*, you'll see that the local media treated our demonstration as a protest rather than a piece of performance art.

Isn't there a flaw in your argument here? The Neoist Alliance appears to be a conspiratorial group and you've recently been writing about the connections between avant-garde movements and secret societies. Doesn't this give critics a good reason to interpret your current activities as being art based?
Not necessarily! Although I'm now interested in connecting the Situationists to secret societies, this largely reflects my obsession with historification and how we understand the past. In this country, the initial reception of the Situationists in the very early sixties was art based. There were discussions and film screenings at the ICA and some coverage in the *TLS* special devoted to the avant-garde. After that, for 30 years the SI had no discernible presence within British cultural institutions. The group didn't generate any press interest in Britain during the mid-sixties, they were more or less ignored beyond very sporadic coverage in the underground press.

Later, the SI were interpreted as a completely political movement by the borderline anarchists who took up their cause. When I first came across the Situationists, they were presented to me as political theorists. According to the assorted ex-public school 'radicals' I encountered in the late seventies, the Situationists had produced the ultimate critique of capitalism. To adopt a peculiarly apt religious phraseology, the SI had 'the answer', their texts were a leftist substitute for the bible. I asked a few pro-situs to tell me what they meant by terms such as 'spectacle' and they either couldn't or wouldn't explain them. I was told I had to read *Society of the Spectacle* and *The Revolution of Everyday Life*. The whole attitude towards the Situationists was a kind of secular Protestantism. When I actually got around to looking through some of the texts, I could see that it was possible to make non-political interpretations of the SI as a group. I went for the artistic line, which at the time was the second most obvious way in which to categorise Situationism. There are, of course, other ways of understanding the group. I was struck by the possibility of an occult interpretation of the SI while reading Nesta Webster's *Secret Societies and Subversive Movements*. She was actually dealing with eighteenth-century freemasons but to me it read like a description of the Situationist International. When I then went and looked at some Situationist texts, they were liberally peppered with secret society references. I'd missed these on previous readings because until recently, I was very dismissive of the occult. I'm more than happy to admit that the Neoist Alliance sprang from the same soil as the Rosicrucians and that this provides a link between my current activities and the Situationist tradition. All I'm doing here is connecting the Neoist Alliance and the SI through the occult, this has nothing to do with Situationism as an art movement. Obviously, I'm not in a position to prevent other people from reinterpreting my recent activities in an art context. I can't control every interpretation of what I do. But I wouldn't see this as a flaw in my thinking.

The way the art world operates seems to have many parallels with secret societies, particularly the activities of avant-garde movements such as Surrealism.

Yes, according to the authors of *The Holy Blood and the Holy Grail,* Cocteau was head of the Priory of Sion.

Are there any connections between the Futurists and Italian Freemasons?

I haven't investigated that at all. I've only been looking into these things since the beginning of the year, which hardly presents enough time to do a serious investigation. Likewise, I don't read Italian, so I wouldn't be the best person to investigate that particular area. In any case, I'm more interested in post-war groups.

The Neoist Alliance is just one area of your practice, could you describe how you use various media to communicate your ideas?

What's crucial to me is the reception of what I'm doing, I'm interested in how people react to it, how they interact with it. Obviously, there are a number of key ideas but how these are put across varies according to the medium I'm using. When I was doing installations in the eighties, one of the things that made them pertinent was actually dealing with the gallery as a space – and not only in an ideological sense. The fact that I was dealing with a physical space was just as important to me. Obviously, there's a vast difference between a gallery and a hole in the road – and this meant there were a lot of ideological issues that had to be dealt with. Among other things, I had to engage with the gallery both as a site of cultural validation and an integral part of the art system. Along with books and essays, the gallery occupies a key position in the process of art historicisation. However, I was also interested in physically messing things up, shining lights in the audience's eyes and generally littering the space. Likewise, I wanted to show that anyone could bullshit their way through the cultural system, that you don't need any specialist training to con money from the British Council. Obviously, a lot of my work took place in what can be described as cyber-space. An example of this would be the attack I launched on traditional notions of identity and creativity by getting several hundred people to use the name Karen Eliot. While critics may or may not want to interpret this project through the prism of post-modernism – and thereby conclude that what I was doing was totally in tune with the times – my main interest was fucking things up.

The Neoist movement was in a sense a parody of an avant-garde group in that it never had one coherent programme, there were multiple programmes, with a tremendous number of references. How do you see Neoism fitting into the so called progression of post-war avant-garde movements, assuming that it does – and if so, how was this or is this to be achieved?

I think a lot of it comes down to what you think the Neoist group was doing. Historifying something means simplifying the elements involved so that they fit a schematic pattern. Taking the Neoists, you've got people like Greil Marcus coming along and saying that Neoism is complete garbage – which is of course true – but Marcus is, as usual, missing the point. The opinions of rival critics are what problematises the process of historification for the various individuals engaged in this cultural practice. Obviously, you've got to sift through the available material and sort out what you want. Neoism, for example, could be interpreted as a modernist movement by privileging the work of Pete Horobin. The whole Data Cell project treated art as more or less a process of administration. In many ways, Horobin's activities ran parallel to – but also parody – the process of historification. He was using rubber stamps and files to document his life as an artist during the ten years from 1980 to 1990, at a time when most businesses had moved on to using computers. The Data project was very bureaucratic and as such appears to be a piece of classic modernism, as long as one resists the temptation to view it as a post-modern pastiche of nostalgia. I think the younger Neoists, John Berndt and myself – Graf Haufen to an extent although his practice was less intellectualised – can be viewed as being completely in tune with the post-modern art of the eighties. However, you can just as easily interpret Neoism as an avant-garde transgression of the modernist/post-modernist project. For the time being, I'd rather leave it to the critics to work out for themselves what Neoism was about. Then, if I don't like what's being said, I'll put some of my own interpretations into the public domain. I'm here to create problems for art historians but before I get into working on this in any big way, the critics will have to do some preliminary work on the raw material.

When you were involved with the Neoists Network, you were obviously aware of what documentation future critics or historians might need in order to perceive this group as historically significant. So you had to go through all the motions of being a proper avant-garde group such as producing manifestos and periodicals, even having internal power struggles.

The power struggles were real enough and I won! When I hooked up with the Neoists, I thought certain aspects of the movement were undeveloped. For example, there wasn't enough text. This was one of the things I wanted to introduce in vast quantities. When I first came across the group, it had existed for several years and the people involved were engaged in a very diverse range of activities. There didn't appear to be any central core to what was going on, Neoism was simply a mass of contradictions. Thus I was able to systematise the group's ideology and slant it in a way that suited me. This was simultaneously accepted as necessary and resented by the people who were involved at the time and even individuals – such as John Berndt – who joined later on, partially as a result of how I'd transformed the group.

Another thing I considered necessary to make Neoism historically viable, was a direct link to Situationism. The early Neoist group had an over linear paternity deriving from a progression through Futurism, Dada, Surrealism, Fluxus and Mail Art. The group lacked any significant input from post-war avant-garde movements such as the SI and Auto-Destructive Art. Although my understanding of the Situationists at that time was not particularly sophisticated because I hadn't read a very representative selection of their writings, I happily chucked bits and pieces plagiarised from their texts into the Neoist manifestos I was concocting. I wanted to transplant the Situationist obsession with text into the Neoist Network because having come out of the Fluxus/Mail Art trajectory, the importance of writing within the avant-garde tradition had been partially lost among my comrades. As a result, the Neoists were in danger of losing their avant-garde identity and becoming just another part of the underground. While its members were madly documenting events, the Neoist Network relied chiefly on visual records and there'd been a failure to grasp the central role written reports played in the process of historicisation. Likewise, for purely economic reasons, a good deal of the documentation the Neoists did produce was substandard in terms of art discourse. Before meeting up with Pete Horobin, I'd never used video or Super 8. At the time of my involvement with Neoism, I wasn't aware of the quality that was required for broadcasting and mass distribution of film and video. A lot of early Neoist documentation fails in terms of high cultural discourse because of its low quality. On the whole, early Neoist attempts at film and video production were abysmal! As I've already said, this was largely due to lack of money. When I was making Super 8 films with Horobin, we were both on the dole, so we'd use out of date film stock that we bought on the cheap from Jessops in Finchley Road.

When I think of a group such as Fluxus, I can picture the photograph in the Silverman collection of the Flux-Shop filled with product. I have seen very little that the Neoists actually produced other than documentation. Does this put a question mark against their possible consideration as an 'important' art movement? Admittedly this factor has not hurt the SI but then even minor Situationists appear more intellectually sophisticated than Neoists such as Istvan Kantor! Is there Neoist material I don't know about?

There are plenty of Neoist works that you don't know about and I assume I'm ignorant of a good many too. Fuck knows how many hundreds of hours of audio works there must be! Likewise, I'm not sure how much text the French-Canadians produced because I've only been able to get my hands on a few fragments of this material. Allegedly, there is considerably more, although I suspect that a lot of this stuff was produced in their post-Neoist phase when they were operating as the Society For The Preservation Of The Future. Obviously, it is problematic to ascribe precise dates to the existence of the Neoist Cultural Conspiracy. As a rough guide, I would describe the period 1977 to 1986 as the Neoist decade. Dave Zack, Al Ackerman and Maris Kundzin fermented the Neoist project at the Portland Academy between 1977 and 1979. Then the virus was transplanted to Montreal, where it went critical and spread world-wide. Between 1980 and 1986, there was at least one Neoist Apartment Festival a year, then a two year gap with no collective actions before the so called Millionth Apartment Festival in New York. There have been no collective manifestations under the aegis of Neoism since 1988, so I think it is fair to assume that as an organised movement, the Neoist Network is dead and buried. Geza Perneczky dealt tolerably well with the question of intellectual sophistication in the chapter on Neoism in his book *A Halo*. As regards a lack of product, I really don't think this is a problem as far as the historical importance of Neoism is concerned. Actually, when I've stayed with individuals such as Pete Horobin, tENTATIVELY a cONVENIENCE, Stiletto and Graf Haufen, I've always been amazed at the profusion of Neoist materials they possess. Even if lack of product was a problem, the work could always be faked up as it was needed! However, as far as I'm concerned, this all rather misses the point. I think that Neoism's relationship to the Plagiarist and Art Strike movements is similar to the role the Lettriste Internationale played with regard to the historically more important Situationist International. Ultimately, Neoism is interesting as a relatively insignificant precursor to a set of far more substantial activities.

You've talked about historification and have said that nobody has done any substantial work on Neoism, but you've written a history of the post-war avant-garde, *The Assault On Culture*. How did you feel about your writing on Neoism then and how would you rewrite it now?

The whole book would be very different if I wrote it again. However, what I have to say about Neoism wouldn't be substantially changed. What you have to understand about that book is that it's organised around the chapter on Neoism. The Neoist Network was what I was most interested in writing about, even if I appeared very dismissive of it. The stuff on the Situationists and Fluxus was simply a way of leading people into a discussion of Neoism. The preamble was necessary because at that time very few people would have been interested in reading a whole book about Neoism. If I wrote the book again today, it would be very different because there is now such a profusion of information about the Situationists and Fluxus. With the Situationists, I'd now place particular emphasis on the occult aspects of their activities. I think received interpretations of the avant-garde are very dull, so I'm forever getting this urge to fuck around with historification, to come up with new and perverse takes on culture. As regards the Fluxus material in *The Assault On Culture*, I'd be less inclined to change it because I don't think the individuals historifying the group have done their work properly. There's no sense of a grand narrative around Fluxus, the movement's history still appears very fragmented. Of course, the average critic would probably say this was good and reflected the work produced by the group. It means, however, that there's no real orthodoxy to kick against. The only thing people writing about Fluxus seem able to agree upon is that the group was somehow of vast importance.

Much work has been done on Gruppe Spur and Viennese Aktionism. The Lettriste Movement is still continuing. There is a mass of information on Isou (mostly written by himself and close associates) but his group has not really caught on like the SI or Fluxus. Do you think there is something to be said for remaining obscure and not really 'playing the game' too much if you want long term critical attention?

In a lot of ways, the SI didn't 'play the game' either. Like the Neoist, Plagiarist and Art Strike movements, the Situationists refused to go straight into galleries. Of course, there are always odd exceptions, such as Istvan Kantor, who has been completely compromised by the art system – but on the whole, the individuals associated with these movements have been playing a cat and mouse game with critics and historians. I've been concentrating on creating something that critics will find alluring, while individuals such as John Berndt and tENTATIVELY a cONVENIENCE have attempted to fuck this up. Of course, I wouldn't want the first critic who comes along to complete the historical packaging of my work. John A. Walker was sniffing about, showing some interest, but I slapped him down in the pages of Variant and that was the end of that – as you can see from his entries on Plagiarism and Neoism in the third edition of *The Glossary Of Art, Architecture and Design Since 1945*. I'm not saying that I've planned every detail of the historicisation of the Neoist, Plagiarist and Art Strike movements. For example, I haven't decided that the ICA must hold a Plagiarist retrospective in 2018. However, I've put a lot of work into structuring these movements so that they can be historically assimilated in the way that I desire. In relation to this, there is certainly something to be said for obscurity because critics and historians like to feel that they've discovered something for themselves. There are reputations to be made from appearing to be the first individual to get into a particular area!

If you're not interested in writing the history of Neoism, do you expect it to happen?
It will happen, it's already happening, historification is an on-going process and I'm busy illustrating how it works. At the moment, I'm writing a novel about the historicisation of Neoism because it's apt that this should occur in a fictional form before too many art historians set to work on it. The novel will also serve to draw critical attention to Neoism.

You make a distinction between underground and avant-garde activities. Do you see novels as more mainstream than gallery culture?
I don't think there is such a thing as mainstream culture, at least not anymore. To use a cliché, we live in a world of proliferating margins. Seriously though, over the past twenty years, we've witnessed an enormous amount of fragmentation going on in both 'serious' and popular culture. The distinction I make between the categories underground and avant-garde is based on the concept of theoretical rigour. Both categories view themselves as oppositional – although this is a claim that I, personally, tend to treat with suspicion – the difference is that the avant-garde is more intellectually vigorous than the underground. Because of this, it is also far more prone to sectarianism.

You've been described as a cult author. Do you see this part of your practice as just underground or do think your fiction is as critically rigorous as your other activities?
I think all modes of discourse tend towards the fictional. To use another cliché, discursive structures simultaneously enable one to speak and limit what can be said. The advantage of using the novel as a form is that it enables me to communicate with various constituencies which are not prepared to listen to the other voices I habitually adopt. But while I consciously rationalise the depiction of sex and violence in my narratives, I'm not interested in the so called 'novel of ideas'. I detest introspection, which is the predominant force shaping literary fiction. I look to genre works for vigour and inspiration. It's also important to me that my novels work as stories, if they didn't, I wouldn't trouble myself with this type of narrative.

In your two published novels, there are scenes which trash art galleries and administrators. Is this a particular obsession of yours? What is your relationship to the art world,

how do you see yourself fitting into it?

With my fiction, there are certain recurring motifs, the destruction of art works is simply one of them. Others include scenes where one or more characters are under the influence of psychedelic drugs. In fact, the most common motifs are scenes of ritualised sex and violence. It's up to the reader to work out what's going on, if I wanted to give a literal explanation of my novels, I wouldn't bother writing works that openly proclaim their status as fiction! As to my relationship with the art world, well, I stand outside it but my work is a Trojan horse that will destroy the existing cultural apparatus once some critic is bold enough to attempt defusing this mimetic time bomb!

Seriously, it seems to me that you have a very detailed knowledge of the art world and that you could actually use this to forge a lucrative career for yourself. Would you ever consider doing this?

Yes, if I was able to do it on my own terms! The basic problem is that I enjoy fucking things up and this isn't how you're supposed to behave within the gallery system. Likewise, I've no real interest in forging an alternative art career that I subsidise from working full time at an art college. Doing something like that would make it very easy for the culture industry to swallow me whole and then exercise an enormous amount of control over my output. I want to be the invisible pilot at the centre of the popular storm, not some dupe afraid to rock the boat because my financial well-being depends on pleasing all the other buffoons toiling within the art system. I've stated elsewhere that 'serious culture' isn't consciously organised as a conspiracy against youth and vigour – but operates as such because 'good taste' dictates that successful artists stick to reproducing an already established ideal.

Do you think it is viable for us to be talking about an avant-garde in the 90s?

Yeah, definitely! I think the very existence of the London Psychogeographical Association proves the viability of the avant-garde in the 90s. Although I was only concerned with producing avant-garde material between 1982 and 1990, I don't think that prevents other individuals taking up the utopian project. While what principally concerns me now is aiding and abetting the historification of the eighties avant-garde, that doesn't stop interested parties taking up the torch passed down through Futurism, Dada, Surrealism, Situationism, Fluxus, Neoism, Plagiarism and the Art Strike. One of the twists I added to the avant-garde tradition was to emphasise the process of packaging movements in preparation for their historification. This was always an important aspect of avant-garde activity. If it hadn't been, the SI wouldn't have bothered depositing vast amounts of material with museums and archives. My achievement was to demonstrate that rather than being recuperated by an all powerful culture industry, avant-garde groups actively collude in the process of art historicisation. I'm sure the rising generation won't have any difficulty in topping this. After all, it wasn't difficult for me to break free from the taints of Fluxus and Situationism.

This ties in with what you've done with the Black Mask book. Rather than publish some new material of your own, you've reprinted little known work that in a way redresses some of the imbalance that's crept into the historicisation of the 60s avant-garde.

One of the points I'm interested in making is that there is no end to the process of historicisation. It's an on-going activity. Most people who've written about the relationship between the Situationists and punk have ignored the Black Mask group and if you're familiar with the relevant material, it makes what's been said on the subject look very silly indeed. Various individuals wanted to portray punk as 'musical Situationism' because the SI needed a stalking horse within popular culture to make them appear hugely influential and thus historically important. In a similar fashion, I'm increasing the viability of the Neoist, Plagiarist and Art Strike movements by citing them as an influence on the KLF and related pop music phenomena.

Aren't you in danger of becoming some kind of high cultural version of Malcolm McLaren's *Great Rock 'n' Roll Swindle?*

If that happens, it will simply illustrate the point I made earlier about the limitations different modes of discourse impose upon what you can say.

Although the idea that punk was a swindle perpetrated on the music industry is completely mythic and bears no relationship to what actually happened, it raises some interesting questions. If we go with the po-mo flow and forget about truth, one of the things we should be asking ourselves is in what ways do various myths promote or hinder social change. It's obvious that the present cultural system benefits a conservative clique, while simultaneously hindering meme mutation and the process of acceleration. For this reason, given the choice between supporting popular taste or defending 'serious culture', I would always take the former option. However, to do this is really to remain locked within the existing system. Having mastered the codes, I'm more interested in destroying the division between high and low brow and creating something new from the resulting wreckage. To conclude with a cliché, until we destroy everything there will only be ruins!

First published in the *Edinburgh Review* number 91, Spring 94

Appendix three

Selected correspondence January to December 1989

To Malcolm Dickson and Pete Horobin 30/1/89

Enclosed is the new *Vague* and various bits of press – you've probably seen most of it before. (…)

We got some money for doing a video for the *Anon* show but I'm not pleased with how it's going. There is a lot of argument around the whole show. Ed puts it down to everyone except himself being petty but actually there's some pretty fundamental disagreements about the nature of the work. Yesterday I had an argument with Ed because he said the gallery was a 'hollow space' which we were going to fill. I found this a bizarre position for someone supposedly making site-specific installation. I ended up saying that if the gallery was just a 'hollow space' then we might as well put the work in a hole in the road.

The *Anon* show may end up looking OK, but I'm pretty disappointed at the way the ideas the show was supposedly about seem to have been abandoned. Anyway, we'll see what happens…

I'm just starting to get on with Art Strike organisation. Things are very well organised over in San Francisco and they had a big *Art Strike Mobilization Week* at the beginning of the month. I've got to get things moving over here…

To Jenny Turner 7/2/89

Got your letter this morning and I'm pleased you're enjoying editing *Pure Mania*. My basic feeling was to let you go through the whole thing and then once you'd sent me a suitably anotated copy of the typescript to use that as a basis for tidying up the text; no doubt I'll make a few alterations of my own as I go through yours. However, I think it's important that some of its 'raw' quality should be retained – although obviously there will be parts of the text which will be all the better for a re-write.

With regard to your questions – read 'sorts' as 'skins' or 'punks' or any other teenage cult. If you substituted another youth cult and the sentence makes sense then it's okay. Page five, yeah, 'pre-sort' as in 'sort' – like 'pre-punk' as in 'punk'. (…)

'Gouts' on page 39 as in drops, the phrase 'spitting out gouts of blood and the occasional piece of broken tooth' is one used by Peter Cave in several of his Hells Angels novels written for New English Library during the seventies. Most of the repeated phrases are sentence used by trash authors – and which they tend to repeat in their novels, although rarely more than once or twice in a single book. (…) The idea of the repetitions is to give the reader a flavour of what it's like to read six or eight formula books by the same author in a day and then repeating this several days running – something which I've done; also such heavy repetition is a way of making this kind of writing deconstruct itself. (...)

Aside from seventies youth culture/exploitation novels, the other main source of reference in *Pure Mania* is to punk – as you've probably spotted, Alienation's career is a loose parody of that of the Sex Pistols and to a lesser extent the Clash. By the way, *Pure Mania* was the title of the Vibrators first lp and the title of a track on their scond album V2. (...)

Enjoyed your piece in the new *Variant.*

To Steve Perkins 7/2/89

I have organised for the *Art Strike Propaganda Workshop* material to be exhibited at Copy Art in London from 10th to 31st May. Can you send me the posters and anything new you want to add as soon as possible please! I've not really discussed this with you but just felt it was best to go ahead with things – I hope you don't think I'm being presumptious.

Enclosed with this are a couple of the texts I'm working on for *Art Strike Handbook.* I felt I had to rework Scott's text. I just wouldn't have been happy publishing it the way it was, although maybe this is a bit unfair of me. Nothing wrong with it as it was, I just wanted to emphasise different things and I'm not saying they're Scott's opinions, he's just the interviewer. Also a short text I've knocked up. I feel the strike aspect of the event needs more emphasis. Sorel is really interesting in relation to this. *Reflections on Violence* is well worth thumbing through, although I wouldn't recommend sitting down and reading straight through it. It's interesting to see how things are developing in different places. Obviously, my angle isn't quite the same as yours and Scott's but I still think there's plenty of common ground. I sent Tony Lowes copies of some of the stuff you sent and he said he'd already got it and was quite enthusiastic. He also mentioned a poor quality audio tape???

Also enclosed Art Strike badges. I'm getting Mark Pawson to do them at cost, and he says he'll do Art Strike badges for you at this incredibly low price if you don't tell anyone he's doing this – or else all his customers will want a discount! I'm also thinking about T-shirts. The leaflet has to be typeset and laid out. I'd like to do about fifty thousand. There's whole streets in London which are part of the Acme Artists Housing Co-op, so it'd be great to go leafleting every house in these streets!

Will probably also hold the *Fifth International Festival of Plagiarism* in Glasgow in late summer. Show in Luton opens on Saturday. Have reformed my band to play at the opening. Been making videos. Have to tidy up my novel – got a letter asking various questions about it from my editor today.

Keep me informed of all Art Strike Action Committe (California) activities. I think there'll be some really interesting developments.

To Joel Biroco 13/2/89

(...) I enjoyed *Smirk* too, but sadly it wasn't one of mine. The guy who did it is called Sam Monk and he has a degree from Oxford and is about twenty-two. I've never met him but I have certain contacts which help me find things like that out. I was thinking of doing a *Smirk* supposedly by Sam Monk which revealed that *Smile* was actually his project and that *Smirk* was just a cheap way of grabbing some attention from *Smile* and himself. Unfortunately, I never got it together as there are always so many things to do. (…)

To Pete Scott AKA Ian Blake 17/2/89

(…) With reference to Kantor, I think you're way off the mark suggesting you've 'probably had more contact with him than anyone else in England'. As far as I know, you've never met him – and there's plenty of people who have. If you take in Scotland, then Horobin is definitely the UK resident who's spent the most time actually sharing spaces with Kantor. I think Horobin, Mark Pawson, Ben Allen, myself and several others all know Kantor better than you – and balanced out have had a lot more 'contact' with him (…)

No wonder you've never understood my differences with Kantor! Your letter says it all: 'He may have monopolized the Monty Cantsin context but that's what it was devised for in the first place (I think)'. To me the whole point of multiple name concepts is that they're to be developed collectively, not monopolised by individuals. Well, at leas you ask: 'Or am I just enacting my usual role as Kantor's apologist?' It's a healthy question to ask but you'll have to answer it yourself, as I don't want to get involved with this issue. (…)

Things are heating up with the Art Strike. It's really well organised in San Francisco and I"m in the process of getting the ball rolling here in London.

To Arthur Berkoff 17/2/89

(…) Glad you found the chapter on Neoism in *Assault on Culture* useful. There's a few ridiculous errors which crept in because when dealing with so many words, I just miss mistakes when checking through, like APT 9 was June '85 and not May '85 as I say. I think I must just have been thinking about APT 8 when I wrote this and put May. (…)

I think it's important to deal with things here and now. My first involvement with Neoism was five years ago, so if I wait another 25 or 30 years before writing about all this stuff it'll be completely different from what I write now. History changes all the time – there's nothing objective about it; so the way I see it, we might as well start writing it now because in 25 years time we'll either be too lazy to write it or we'll just write something completely different anyway – so it doesn't really matter. We can write one thing now and something else in 25 years time. Anyway, I left Neoism four years ago. So for me it's over…

I agree with you about the *Village Voice* piece though. This type of journalism is a real problem. Of course, I've my own axe to grind because it misrepresents *Smile* on the basis of an issue that came out three years before the article was written, but generally too I think this is a very bad piece of writing.

To Steve Perkins 24/2/89

Your latest package was the best thing I've got through the post in ages. Loved the *Art Strike Propaganda* posters; the way they were slapped together with real speed and energy… I was hoping to have the press release written for the show I'm making of them to send to you with this. But I've been so tied up with a lot of mundane things that it looks like

I'll have to write it when I get back from New York. I like to be ahead of myself but there is still plenty of time to publicise that show once I get back to London at the end of March. (...)

Enjoyed Janet's Art Strike bit, it's really true, the Art Strike is so many different things. I've been making copies of the piece from *Coming Up!* and sending those out. Also been sending asnd giving out badges. Tony Lowes has reworked his *Give Up Art* leaflet so there's mention of the Strike at the end of it. He seems quite keen on the whole thing and is doing his bit to promote it. I've been working on getting people like Graf Haufen and Arthur Berkoff interested. I'm sure John Berndt will do his bit in Baltimore. (...) I'm planning to picket the Association of Art Historians conference once I get back here. Hopefully the leaflet will be ready for that. Also, I'm going to leaflet all the streets I know which have a really high proportion of artists living in them. (...)

To Peter Suchin 24/2/89

Thanks for your letter and list of corrections. Good of you to take the trouble of writing them out. Amerika was a deliberate deviation but on the whole the book suffered from insufficient proof reading and the fact that my final corrections were never made to the damn thing before it was desk-top published on a machine someone had access to while their boss wasn't looking. Polygon, who're publishing a novel by me later this year, have expressed a vague interest in reprinting the book. They seem to want me to write a follow up novel and then think about revising AOC.

Anyway, enclosed with this are copies of all the published reviews I know of that AOC has received – and also the majority of other press that I've received over recent years. Obviously a lot of this stuff is pretty inaccurate; for example Stefan Szczelkun organised *Ruins of Glamour* installation not Art In Ruins, Ed Baxter and myself organised *Desire in Ruins* not Art In Ruins (and incidently, contrary to popular belief the titles of these shows were not suggested by Art In Ruins, but by others participating in the installations) – similarly Istvan Kantor has at various times managed to get himself credited with an awful lot of work actually executed either collectively or else with which he has no involvement whatsoever (the *New Art Examiner* review of *Smile* is completely inaccurate because Grant Kester was fed bum information by a Neoist irritated by the fact that the only 'Neoist' material he could interest Kester in was stuff that I'd done, so he gave Kester the impression that 'my' work had been executed by a variety of Neoists and Neoist offshoots).

I have only just got the new *Here and Now* and want to finish reading the whole magazine before writing a reply to the stuff in it. I won't get down to doing this until after I get back from New York at the end of March. I thought your letter was very reasonable. Obviously I hadn't seen the *Destruction of Art as an Institution* piece when I wrote my letter. Incidently, that letter was just intended as a personal letter to Keith and Alastair – it was never intended for publication. (...)

To Steve Perkins 24/3/89

(...) I just got back from New York yesterday (...) The USA was really great. I was there for three weeks. Two and a half in New York and four days in the middle in Baltimore with TENTATIVELY A CONVENIENCE, Laura Trussell, John Berndt and various other ex-Neoists and Krononauts (…)

Among many others, I met Billy Name at the Dick Higgins opening – Tom, the guy I was staying with, and I took him to a party for Susan Hiller at Pat Hearn's apartment. Billy felt out of place so he split (…) Lynne Tillman was there and she was really nice (…) Afterwards we went to EAT with Claudia Hart – this was really funny because Claudia Hart kept asking me what I thought of different people's work and I hadn't heard of half the people she asked me about; and she couldn't believe it when I just said straight to her that I wasn't familiar with this stuff, that I had no interest in the 'mainstream' art world. She kept wanting to know if I was one of 'them', which turned out to be a 'mainstream' (to me but I guess not to her) cultural leftist (…)

Saw all Nick Zedd's films, they were great although he wasn't particularly inspired when talking about them. I like the way he undercuts traditional notions of gender by playing female roles himself (…) *Whoregasm*, which has split screen projection is definitely his best film. It's pretty psychedelic. The talk he gave afterwards was really bad. People kept standing up and saying he owed them money or made cryptic references to him being a junkie (…)

Went down to the Anarchist Switchboard and met various people there but the politics didn't seem to go beyond 'Off The Pigs' and talk of last years Tompkins Park riot. A lot of the people around the switchboard seemed pretty bombed out – the whole scene seemed very similar to the anarcho-squatting scene in London (…)

Ralph Rumney was just on the 'phone. I just managed to catch his retrospective at England & Co. on my way back from the airport – it was only on for three weeks. It included stuff from his show at Transmission (…)

To Sean Bowen 26/3/89

Dear Sean

(…) the whole point about Art Strike is to wind artists up. To bring the idea of the class war into the cultural realm. Of course I don't expect artists to want to take part but I can use the idea of the Art Strike to illuminate the divide between art (which is reactionary) and radical (in)action (…)

Richard Allen is the pen name of James Moffatt. As Richard Allen, Moffatt wrote a series of cult books with titles like *Skinhead*, *Suedehead*, *Boot Boys*, *Knuckle Girls* &c. They're a big influence on my writing – although they're basically written from a right/racist position, a perspective I don't share. But the prose style is really great. You should check them out in your secondhand bookstore, Oxfam, or wherever. I wrote a piece about Moffatt in the *Smile* section of *Vague* 20 *Televisionaries.*

To Steve Perkins 3/4/89

Thanks for your letter and the AS stuff. It's good to get this stuff. I seem to have lost Scott's address – although I'm sure it will turn up somewhere, so for the time being you're my only contact with AS CA. I have the box number, who actually collects the stuff from there??

I finally got a leaflet printed. I've sent a copy separately with the latest *Variant.* I leafleted the party for the closing of the

Air Gallery on Friday 31st March. Seemed to get a reasonably good reaction. Interest and a certain amount of disbelief. I've also been doing door to door leafleting in areas known to have high concentrations of artists/squatters &c. I've done Grays Inn Buildings, Bonnington Square, St. Agnes Place, Pullins Estate. I've yet to do Colville Road and Beck Road which have a lot of Acme houses in them (artists housing co-op). On Thursday, I'm organising a small picket to leaflet the 15th Annual Conference of the Association of Art Historians. Here, one of the things needed is just getting the information out. Basically just getting as many people as possible to know about it.

Another idea I had – which I wasn't going to attempt to put into practice until later in the year – was to try and get hold of headed paper from institutions like ICA, Tate, MOMA, and send out forged press releases saying that as of January 1st 1990 they'd be closing down for three years in support of the Art Strike. The Art Workers Coalition pulled a similar stunt in the late sixties and it seemed to work quite well.

Also, it'll help once I've got this damn typesetting sorted out and can get out the *Art Strike Handbook* and *Festival of Plagiarism* documentation. Then I'll have something a bit more in-depth to send people who express interest in the leaflet. Also, I'll probably do a follow up leaflet in a few months. At the moment, I'm working on publicity for the exhibition of AS propaganda at Copy Art. Have to send out the press release today. We're having a propaganda workshop on May 20th and maybe that'll also generate some more ideas.

Thought your Plagiarism statement was well balanced, showing both good and bad sides of the event. Hope you get inspired with some new way of engaging in AS because you're probably the person in SF who is most in tune with my way of thinking about it. One of the reasons I like leafleting is because it's totally divorced the whole thing from any gallery set up.

To John Berndt 12/4/89

Thanks for mailing that package of stuff and your letter. I really enjoyed my trip to the States and it was good to see you and tent. I thought New York was fantastic (…)

I'm having a very frustrating time getting the typesetting done for *Festival of Plagiarism* documentation and *Art Strike Handbook*. Ed Baxter was supposed to do it while I was in the States – and this was about the third arrangement I'd made to get it done – but having read it, he refused to do it. Now Erica is supposed to be doing it but there's been a problem with downloading it. I can't believe how much this stuff has been delayed – it should have been out at the end of January, but I'll get it out eventually.

My plans for the Art Strike include doing a leaflet encouraging museum guards to go on strike so that art galleries and museums have to be closed because there's no one to look after the exhibits.

I went to Paris over the weekend and stayed with Sevol. The main purpose of this trip was to do an interview with Ralph Rumney around the Situationist exhibition for *Art Monthly* and see RU. Nothing spectacular to report about it. It was quite tiring and annoying I couldn't spend more time with RU and Ellie, but that's the way it goes.

To William Clark 8/5/89

A few further thoughts on the *Festival of Plagiarism*. I think it'd be nice to close with music on the Friday night as well as having it on the Sunday if we can get a PA free or very cheap, as long as you don't think this is going to cause you too much work. The Sunday could then be given over to more experimental music and the Friday could be rockist with my band, Jayne's band (I heard a tape and thought they were great!) and this total plagiarist band I saw on Thursday night in Glasgow called the Kolostomy Bags (I've probably spelt the name wrongly), they're friends of Jayne's and really great.

I though Monday evening should be given over to anarchist video, I've been chasing some things up today and will be able to sort this out myself.

We'll have a better idea of what other things there'll be once I get back from Germany. Also, it's important for you to send out your mailing with the leaflets as soon as possible. It's just a matter of getting the information around.

Don't forget to mail me a plan of the gallery as soon as possible. Thanks for all your help.

To Charlton Burch 11/5/89

It was great to get the new copy of *Lightworks* (…) I was obviously very pleased to see my piece appear and overall more than happy with the editing job you'd done on it. Indeed, I was very impressed with your subtitling and the way you broke the article down into smaller paragraphs. However, I would like to make a couple of points in case any correspondence arises over the article.

1 Under the subheading *Smile Begins*, (second paragraph, seventh line) your edit reads: 'By the time I came across the name (Monty Cantsin), I was the only one using it.' This is factually incorrect. The draft I sent you read: 'By the time I came across it, only one person was using it' (i.e. the Monty Cantsin name). I realise this sentence was a bit clumsy and needed re-writing but by one person using the name, I meant someone other than myself because – obviously – I had to come across the name and the concept behind it before I could start using it.

2 Even more trivial than my first point, you've taken out a number of qualifications from the draft I sent you. So, for example, 'the name Karen Eliot briefly became over identified with me' becomes 'the name Karen Eliot became identified with me'. I feel the sense here is changed from a lot of people thought I was doing more with the name than anyone else (at least this was the meaning I was aiming to achieve when I wrote the sentence), to everyone thought I was Karen Eliot. Obviously the change in meaning is fairly subtle, but given the subject matter I feel it's important.

Anyway, I just wanted to clear up these points in case anyone wrote to you about the article. Obviously, I'd consider it a waste of space to take up column inches in the next issue going over the matter. I'm very pleased you carried the piece and don't imagine these very minor points will be of interest to more than a handful of people (…)

To Tom McGlynn 19/5/89

(…) At the moment I've got *Demolish Serious Culture* on at Copy Art, it's all Art Strike propaganda from California. I just organised the show. The opening was really great. Tomorrow we've got a propaganda workshop.

Next week I'm doing a lecture on the Art Strike at City of London Polytechnic. So the propaganda's getting around.

Of course, I haven't heard from a lot of the people I met in New York who said they were going to send me things but that's what you expect. However, I got a couple of books from Lynne Tillman and a really nice card. Her writing's really great. (…)

To Steve Perkins 31/5/89

Thanks for yr latest package. I loved the Carl Andre card and I'm tempted to do a leaflet entitled *Let them eat Bricks* in reply – sure it's a cheap shot but why not? (…) It should upset the art establishment (in NY anyway). Apparently an anti-Art Strike group is in the process of forming in Baltimore, so John Berndt must have been putting lots of energy into his propaganda efforts (…)

I really liked your detournement of *Anarchist*, changing the gender has a serious effect on its impact. It's a great idea to write to institutions with an Art Strike proposal, just to get a response and their headed paper. Maybe we could suggest to all large museums that they close one gallery for the duration of the Art Strike, with a sign put up to inform the public about this.

With the Plagiarism documentation I didn't have enough information to write much about events in SF or Madison. I'm still looking forward to seeing your documentation of SF. I know nothing at all about what happened in Madison – I've not heard from Xexoxial Endarchy since the end of 1987. I have, of course, sent them the two booklets.

Anyway, I'm off to Berlin for two weeks tomorrow.

To Karen Goaman 31/5/89

Thanks for sending me a copy of the upgrading proposal. I've only had time to read it once very quickly and I'll be making these comments from memory as I don't want to go through it now – I don't have much time.

Overall I had no problems with what you say – although I'm never going to be 100% in agreement with how someone else describes what I do. I think it would be unrealistic to even hope for such a state of affairs.

A few points which don't necessarily mean you've misquoted me – maybe I was just slack in expressing myself:

To me the use of the term pro-Situ implies a basic agreement with the ideas of the Debordist faction of the Situationist International. I'm not sure what context I might have used it in – but rather than wishing to distinguish myself from just 'pro-Situs', I'd prefer to distinguish myself from Situationists per se.

I'm not really happy with the idea that I stopped working with Hannah and Glyn because of 'their egotism' and problems of age difference. The whole issue was far more complex than this. I think we were working in fundamentally different ways and we quickly exhausted the common ground between us and had learnt all we were going to learn from each other. I did find H & G difficult to work with but to attribute this simply to egotism misses the point – I don't actually know anyone who isn't egotistical. Similarly, I don't particularly disapprove of them exhibiting in commercial art galleries, it's what they do in these and their general attitude towards their work and their audience &c., which I consider more important. I don't think the age differences were particularly important either – I sometimes found them condescending but this didn't seem to me to have anything to do with age. The piece you reproduce from their catalogue is something they put together from two different pieces of my writing and with which I'm not particularly happy. Finally, you should bear in mind that Simon's relationship with them was always very different from mine because he'd been their student and they'd supported him against the authorities at Kingston Polytechnic (…)

To tENTATIVELY a cONVENIENCE 21/6/89

Thanks for your letter and the Art Strike piece which I will probably use somewhere quite soon (…) It's actually amazing what threatens people. That's why I've kept going with the Art Strike thing – because people do get very very upset about it. The Californian Art Strike Action Committee recently had a card from Carl Andre denouncing it (…)

I was in Berlin for two weeks which was great. I stayed with Graf Haufen and saw Stiletto, Kerstain, Franz John &c. (…) The feeling in Berlin about Neoism is the same as it is here, that it's all over. That was also the vibe I picked up from you and John while I was in Baltimore, the so called *Millionth Apt* seems to have pissed everyone off, Stiletto certainly wasn't very impressed by it.

I'm taking part in a panel talk at the Institute Of Contemporary Arts on the Situationists on Saturday. The whole thing is getting very ridiculous. It all seems very disorganised and my intention is to be pretty negative – I'm supposed to be discussing the recuperation of the Situationists but what I'll say runs along the lines of there was never anything to recuperate (…)

To Pete Horobin 21/6/89

(…) I was in Berlin for the first two weeks of this month staying with Graf Haufen. He now runs a video store with Inus and his main interest is gore and sleaze films. He has an amazing and very massive private collection of film on video as well as the stuff he rents out at the store. While I was there I watched quite a bit of stuff – including *Cannibal Holocaust*, *Ilsa She Wolf of the SS*, *Faces of Death* &c. He'd also organised a season of Doris Wishman movies at an alternative cinema and so I saw *Deadly Weapons*, *Double Agent 73*, *Bad Girls go to Hell* (…)

To Steve Perkins 2/7/89

(…) Did I tell you the Art Strike show went on to Lee House, an anarchist community centre in Stoke Newington? It was on show there for most of last month. I will take it up to Glasgow to show during the *Festival of Plagiarism*. Talking of which, I'm still looking forward to seeing the SF FOP documentation (…)

To Arthur Berkoff 2/7/89

(…) Vis a vis the tape, as far as I'm concerned, Neoism is over and this would also seem to be the attitude of John Berndt, tentatively, Graf Haufen, Stiletto &c., all of whom I've spent time with this year.

Kantor is totally out of touch with what I do. For one thing, it wouldn't matter whether I made video and music or not, I could still make judgements about Neoism – as it happens, I've been making music for the last ten years and have made odd bits of video over the last five years. Anyway, I am very clear about the fact that art is a subset of various categories such as music, painting, writing &c. On the tape Kantor suggests I think art is just objects sold for money, this is so ridiculous I'm not going to waste my time engaging with his 'arguments'.

Anyway, it sounds like you had a good time in the States. I'm looking forward to the FESTIVAL OF PLAGIARISM in Glasgow.

To Freddie Baer 16/8/89

(...) Glasgow was good, *Festival of Plagiarism* went very well (...) Good to finally get a UK screening for *Decoder.* It's crazy that it's never been shown here before. Also showed it in London at the Scala, the day after the Festival ended in Glasgow. The place was packed (...)

To Kim Davis 16/8/89

Thanks for your letter, I'm glad you liked *Assault on Culture*. Yeah, I partially wanted to wind up pro-situs but I also happen to think Richard Allen is well hard. I'm not the only one either, people like Jon Savage also think he was an influence on punk.

Of course, I'm well aware that James Moffatt who wrote the skinhead books under the Allen pen-name was forty-eight when the first one came out and so they weren't exactly written from participant observation. He was a Canadian immigrant to boot, so that accounts for a few of the sillier obsessions, however I still think the voice in the books comes across as very surprisingly and authentically English.

The Kids isn't worth a light next to any of Moffatt's stuff (as well as Richard Allen he also wrote under his own name and as J. J. More). You can spot a mile off that Tony Parsons had pretensions about being something more than a hack. I don't have a copy of THE KIDS to hand, a shame because I like it, but I still think the end is a give-away about where Parsons is going, the last line is something like 'He was looking for something'. Moffatt would never end with something as arty-farty as that. That's also why the Allen books are ultimately better than any of the Hells Angels books – despite the fact that both Peter Cave and Mick Norman wrote better sex and violence – Moffatt's best books are filled with this grinding pessimism. And even his worst books have odd passages of very smart description. Admittedly, the Johnny Canuck books he wrote in the sixties are utter shite, but everything from the seventies has at least something to make it worth reading (...)

To tENTATIVELY a cONVENIENCE 8/9/89

Dear tent

(...) I'm trying to crank a few things out before the end of the year. Main thing is working on a new novel. The first one has been delayed and will now be published in November this year. Also, I'm getting a ridiculous amount of offers of work writing for other magazines. *Assault on Culture* seems to have caught up with me and as a result a lot of small, badly paying, magazines want 'original' commissioned pieces from me. A strange situation. Mainly I don't have time for this or the offers of teaching

I'm getting at the moment. Funny how it all worked out exactly as I planned five years ago – create a big demand for my stuff just before I go on strike.

Festival of Plagiarism in Glasgow was really great. Very relaxed, although a lot of hard work for me. Created a lot of interest. A good social event with lots of interesting discussions and a decent theoretical base to work from. Main disappointment was that Horobin didn't turn up at all. He could have easily camped outside Glasgow and got into the city in half an hour, or even just come in for a day, but he was determined not to take part (...).

To Pete Scott AKA Ian Blake 8/9/89

(...) I haven't had a chance to view the *Ratbag/Black Stigmata* video yet. Mark Pawson was winding you up saying that your *Smile* video was shown at an evening introduced by Genesis P. We did show the video on a monitor in the foyer of the Scala when Tom, James Mannox and myself organised a screening of *Decoder* in London but Genesis P. was not at the event. So it is true to say it got screened at the Scala in the interval between features along with some other stuff. It was also shown twice during the *Festival of Plagiarism*, Pawson got it put on as part of the Psychic Youth night but without sound and I just put it on by itself (...)

To Steve Perkins 8/9/89

Thanks for your letter and the five dollar bill which wasn't necessary but gratefully received none the less. Graf Haufen did an Art Strike exhibition in Berlin but the idea doesn't seem to have inspired anyone to set up an Action Committee on mainland Europe. I notice the propaganda seems to get around, but there's the whole problem of language barriers, so it seems more or less to have been reduced to a slogan in non-English speaking parts of Europe.

I've not heard from Geza Perneczky for ages. He said he was going to send me some kind of critical letter about my attitude to Neoism but I have yet to receive it. I thought he was doing a general book about the Network. I didn't know he was doing a research project focused specifically on Neoism (...)

I don't have anything new to send you on the Art Strike for inclusion in your pamphlet. I keep thinking I should write something about why the New York Art Strike over the bombing of Hanoi was reactionary but haven't got it together. You know the issues, treating art as having value and withholding that value. It was all very tied up with Art Workers Coalition and that crowd. Unless I can get something critical written, it seems best to ignore it because the only thing it has in common with our Art Strike is the name, it had nothing to do with attacking art as an elitist discourse.

Anyway, it's good you're getting out a pamphlet because my *Art Strike Handbook* has no distribution in the States at all. I was thinking of shipping you some copies but it seems better for you to do something specifically designed for the US.

To Bob Black 16/9/89

Tom Vague kindly made me a copy of your latest 'critique' of *The Assault On Culture.* I have a few points to make in relation to it which I hope will be of interest to you (...) It's rather unfortunate that you seem to have missed the fact that I never intended Assault to be read as a considered study of utopianism. I thought I'd made it clear that the book was a partial history of a set of phenomena that I'd labelled utopian and which, apart for some introductory comments, spanned a forty year period (beginning on 8th January 1946 with the founding of Lettrisme in Paris and ending in Berlin on 7th December 1986 at the close of the 64th Neoist Apartment Festival). The emphasis I placed on my engagement with the subject was intended to impress upon the reader the fact that the text was anything but a balanced (or objective) overview of latter day utopianism – and that, when all was said and done, what held the material together was a combination of my interest in it and its debt to the influence of Futurism and Dada. As I write in the introduction:

'After the event, it is easy enough to perceive a tradition running from the Free Spirit, through the writings of Winstanley, Coppe, Sade, Fourier, Lautreamont, William Morris, Alfred Jarry, and on into Futurism and Dada – then via Surrealism into Lettrisme, the various Situationist Movements, Fluxus, 'Mail Art', Punk Rock, Neoism and contemporary anarchist cults. Taking this as our hypothesis – we will not trouble ourselves over whether such a perspective is 'historically correct' – we will construct a 'meaningful' story from these fragments.'

In my opinion, history is anything but an objective discipline, which is why I felt free to include jokes and provocations as well as 'hard facts' in what I hoped would be an entertaining (as well as an informative) book. It would be ridiculous if, for example, I attempted to defend my comments on the surrealists (two or three sentences in the introduction) as a serious critique – I included them to infuriate the vast army of pompous fans who've grown up around this group.

I find it rather difficult to take Hegel, dialectics, and much of the other intellectual baggage which accumulates in the course of your 'critique' very seriously. Similarly, I'm indifferent as to whether or not I'm a 'revolutionary' or a 'materialist', In *Assault* I was parodying a specto-Situationist obsession by emphasising the 'materialist' nature of particular ideas. And while ideologues as diverse as stalinists, left communists, class struggle anarchists and third position fascists are obsessed with proving that they alone are worthy of the description revolutionary, I'm more interested in sticking two fingers up at the wankers who indulge in this posturing (…)

Your admission that: 'The sits… probably should be taken down a peg or two…' rings hollow when contrasted to the way in which you attempt to debunk my (largely borrowed) criticisms of their theory. Strike one: the argument I advance against Debord could just as easily be used against Marx (which is hardly surprising in view of the fact that Debord modelled the concept of the spectacle on Marx's treatment of capital). As you ought to know, Marx isn't beyond criticism, in fact he's as liable to error as any other author and as such his work has been subject to refutation from both the left and the right. Strike two: you accuse me of indulging in the very (un)theoretical practices which I criticise in others. While I may well be a hypocrite, this 'fact' doesn't invalidate the arguments I advance against Debord. Strike three: you ignore the really tricky points I raise (such as the fact that the recessions of the seventies demonstrated that specto-Situationist analysis – based as it was upon the belief that capitalism had overcome its economic contradictions – was incorrect) while pretending you've dealt with all my objections (...)

Your claim that I'm Anglocentric 'when circumstances permit' doesn't hold water. To make a solid case you need to explain why I don't devote chapters to such London centred phenomena as Project Sigma, King Mob, the Angry Brigade, Oi!, the Neo-Naturists &c. Project Sigma is particularly pertinent. If I'd used the selection criteria you claim I adopted in choosing what went into *The Assault On Culture*, then Sigma would have formed the central core of the book. As I presume you know, Sigma was a London centred movement founded by Alexander Trocchi, a former British member of the Lettriste and Situationist Internationals. However, rather than devoting space to Trocchi, I wrote about the 2nd Situationist International, which didn't contain any British members whatsoever!. (...)

While there is a bias in favour of European (and in particular Northern European) material in *Assault*, there is an equally clear bias in favour of North American material in the selection of contemporary texts for the *Rants* book which you co-edited with Adam Parfrey. However, I didn't work myself into a tizzy because you didn't include Tom Vague, Dermot Todd, Mark Downham, God Told Me To Do It, John Nicolson, Anastasia, Billy Childish, Maxim Decharne, Frank Key, John Michell, Dedwydd Jones, John Barker (Jimmy Wild), Paul Sieveking, the Pleasure Tendency, Farquhar McLay, the Wise brothers &c. I select material on the basis of what interests me and I presumed you did the same. That people are usually most interested in what they've experienced first hand has never surprised me. What amazes me is the way in which you arbitrarily link this to nationalism. For example, you claim that: 'Home doesn't – can't – deal with counter-cultural currents however important that don't activate his nationalism. I've mentioned SF fandom and related currents.' But since SF is an international phenomenon what this actually reveals are your own imperialist tendencies, your desire to claim everything that's 'good and true' as American. The reason I don't write about SF isn't because it doesn't exist in England (it does) but because it doesn't interest me. In my letter to Factsheet Five, I highlighted similar chauvinism on your part pertaining to Fluxus, Mail Art and Neoism. Despite these criticisms, you continue to claim and/or imply that various transatlantic phenomenon are solely North American affairs. For example, 'The Canadian and American Neoists have repeatedly trekked to London... If a tendency impinges on England, Home gives it a bit of publicity.' By placing emphasis on the handful of American and Canadian Neoists who've been to London (usually for a holiday and rarely more than once), you give the impression that Neoism was principally a North American phenomenon which 'impinged' upon the UK. However, and as you know, there was an indigenous Neoist scene in Britain (not to mention other parts of Europe) which operated quite autonomously of the North American network (...)

As regards the specto-SI's influence on May '68, David Dunbar makes an interesting point in his essay 'The Picturesque Ruins of the Situationist International' (*Performance Magazine* no. 58, London Summer '89): 'If the activities of the SI really did possess the power to provoke a potentially revolutionary general strike… then an individual with the tastes of Debord would have continued to provoke such strikes until the outbreak of proletarian revolution.' And for an example of the right exaggerating the role of the specto-SI in the May events, I refer you to a televised speech given by de Gaulle on 7/6/68 and cited by Ken Knabb in his *The Blind Men and the Elephant: selected opinions on the Situationists*: 'This explosion was provoked by a few groups in revolt against modern society, against consumer society, against technological society, whether communist in the East or capitalist in the West – groups, moreover, that do not know what they would put in its place, but that delight in negation, destruction, violence, anarchy, brandishing the black flag.' I presume it's obvious to you that the right wanted to place the blame for the May events on a handful of trouble makers because to admit anything else would have been tantamount to confessing that there was no legitimacy in their rule over the French people (…)

Your claim that the specto-Situationists 'must have had many sympathisers for their slogans to have been spray painted all over Paris', is utterly specious. Even if I accept your assertion that their slogans were to be found all over the French capital, the graffiti could easily have been the work of two or three individuals undertaking a systematic propaganda campaign. You claim in the very sentence I've quoted from that the specto-Situationists had thrown 'themselves into an immense project of agitation'. It must have been an immense project indeed, for as Enrage (and later official member of the specto-SI) Rene Vienet admitted in his book about May '68, the specto-SI AND its Enrage supporters in Paris at the time ran to the grand total of 40! As a result, I have little sympathy for your claim that it is 'common knowledge (sic) that the Enrage student allies of the Situationists provoked an escalating series of confrontations with university and police authorities which eventuated in a general strike by ten million workers.' As I understood it, the March 22nd Movement provoked an escalating series of confrontations with university and police authorities. The reason these met with success was due to widespread opposition to the Fouchet Plan for the rationalisation of the education system. The workers came out on strike largely in opposition to the Fifth Plan (a scheme to perfect the French economy by encouraging concentration of industry allowing Capital to control salaried workers, and maintaining a pool of unemployed potential scabs). All of this had very little to do with the specto-SI – and if the May events can be said to have a leader then it is undoubtedly Daniel Cohn-Bendit (who the specto-Situationists cast as one of their arch-rivals, presumably out of jealousy) (…)

To Peter Kravitz 27/9/89

Thanks for getting the proofs to me at last (…) I got a great rejection letter from Giles O'Bryen at Fourth Estate the other day: 'I see I've had your book *Pure Mania* for over a year, which must make you the most patient man on earth.

Worse still, when I read it I didn't really like it that much so am not going to offer to publish it. If you ever get the chance to spit on my grave, seize it!' (…)

Judith Squires rang up two days ago and she wants me to do a discussion about Art Strike at the ICA. So that'll take place on 13th or 14th December. (…)

To Peter Suchin 27/9/89

Enclosed are a few things you could use in the next *H&N*. The review of *Lipstick Traces* was originally done for *New Art Examiner* (they asked me to do it) but I'm not certain they're going to use it now as they seem to be trying to get me to write out the connections I make between art and class. For example, where I use the phrase 'the class basis of culture', they've suggested what I mean would be clearer to their readers (sic) if I wrote 'the class basis of punk culture'. The general drift of what they'd like me to write seems to be that popular culture is class based while art rises above these petty divisions!

Anyway, even if the piece was used in *H&N* and *NAE*, I don't think there'd be much overlap in readership. I also enclose Bob Black's latest diatribe against *Assault* and my reply. The two of these together are probably a bit long for *H&N* – indeed Black's piece on its own is far too long. Anyway, if you want to use them you can (…) I've also sent these things to Peter Kravitz at *Edinburgh Review* because he expressed an interest after Ed Baxter mentioned Black's thing to him. Ed at first told me he thought there was something to be said for Black's argument and then, after I pointed out a few of the more glaring errors, seemed to change his mind. It's pathetic that so called left intellectuals like Black and John A. Walker should resort to attempting to refute arguments I advance on the grounds that they could be advanced against Marx. No doubt these wankers would enforce *Das Kapital* as Holy Writ if they ever gained power in a revolutionary (sic) situation.

To Lynne Tillman 14/10/89

(…) I'm quite curious about how you write, I just bang all my fiction straight onto the word processor – although with reviews and critical pieces I sometimes make notes first. With the book I'm working on, I just roughed out a page of plot, wrote down the names of the main characters and set to work. With fiction I feel it's okay to just make it up as I go along. I know I want certain characters and I know I want certain things to happen but it's not always clear until I'm part of the way into the story exactly who's going to do what. I sometimes make elaborate plots in my head but I can't see the point of putting them into the computer as detailed plans because they always change so much once I start to write them. I find it much better to hammer it out and knock the ms into shape on the rewrite (…)

To Peter Suchin 8/11/89

I saw Gus the evening you wrote your letter, so I'm catching up a bit on what's happening with H&N. No problem about not being able to use the Black stuff, I thought it was probably too long. I'll try and enclose a second round of it with this. I'm having no more communication with Black – I think this new exchange shows fairly conclusively that he's a time waster (…)

The ICA talk now appears to be solely me and Alan Sinfield although there was mention early on of getting Mike Peters and I tried to persuade them to get Jean Gimpel, Roger Taylor and/or Gustav Metzger. Anyway, the talk will be on December 7th at 7.30pm.

I'd not seen the reference to my talk on the Situationists in *Modern Painters*, so thanks for that and your letter about it. I'm not actually going to write to them myself. (...)

I've finished the first draft of my new novel and I've now got to work my arse off revising it before the end of the year. I'll be really pleased to go on strike!

To Edward Ball 25/12/89

Thanks for you card. I haven't actually heard from the people you mention but have ended up going on national radio and London tv to talk about the Art Strike in the past couple of weeks. The Irish branch of the Art Strike were on Eire national radio again last month. The talk at the ICA went very well. A much better atmosphere than is usually to be found there. Of course, the problem is the event only really attracted people who were sympathetic to the idea. The CA Art Strike Action Committee told me they got a lot of mail as a result of your piece in the *Voice*.

Had the launch of my novel 11 days ago and that also went well (...)

To Steve Perkins 25/12/89

Thanks for the *Plagiarism* documentation. It looks great and contains enough information to give people a good idea of what happened. I can't face doing a piece about Glasgow which is as exhaustive as my piece about London. So for the next three years at least, the little piece you got off me on Glasgow is the last word I'll have to say on the subject (...) I'm really going to drop everything after the next seven days. We'll keep the ASAC (UK) box open but only send out material put together before 1/1/90 – including standardised letters that I'll compose in a day or two (...)

To Tom McGlynn 25/12/89

I've been meaning to write for about four months but I've been so damn busy. My novel came out about two weeks ago (...) *The Festival of Plagiarism* in Glasgow went really well. But I forgot to take your golden calf with me, so it didn't get smashed up. I was really going to do that performance and I was so rushed before I went that I forgot to take the one vital element. Anyway, it still looks good in my flat (...) I've finished another novel so the publishers have something to keep them going for the next three years.

Ed seems okay, Andy and Simon too. I passed Hannah and Glyn the other day. I said hello to them, they don't speak to me now anyway and didn't reply but I was quite glad really because they looked incredibly depressed and totally exhausted. They looked in really bad shape (...)

To whom it may concern

Thanks for your communication. For the period 1/1/90 to 1/1/93 the Art Strike Action Committee (UK) will not be producing or circulating any new material. We're not seeking to promote the Art Strike during this period but will continue to supply texts published prior to 1/1/90 to those who send us an SAE or IRCs.

As well as a variety of free leaflets and press cuttings, the following publications are still available from us:

Smile 11	30p
Festival of Plagiarism	£1.95
Art Strike Handbook	£1.95

Post free in the UK

Outside the UK add £1 postage for the first two items ordered and 50p for every two items after that. Cheques payable to S. Home. Cheques must be in sterling and drawn on a London bank. If sending cash from abroad pay only in sterling or US dollars.

If this letter fails to answer any questions you might have please write again after 1/1/93 when we will resume personal correspondence.

Appendix four

Introduction to the Polish edition of the Assault on Culture

ANYONE WHO IS UNFAMILIAR with the subject matter of this book would be best advised to read this new introduction after they have perused the 'original' text. While I am very pleased to see the work translated into Polish, I would write something completely different if I were to sit down again and compose a treatise on the movements that are described in the following pages. The book was written towards the end of 1987 and published in the summer of 1988, at a time when it was difficult for English readers to obtain information on groups such as the Situationists and Fluxus. Since then, there have been major retrospective exhibitions devoted to both these movements and the publication of numerous catalogues. Two further monographs have appeared on the Situationists in English, two in French and one in German. A good deal of previously untranslated Situationist material has recently been published in English and the craze for such books shows no sign of abating,

While Anglo-American cultural historians now seem happy to treat Fluxus and the Situationist International (SI) as the most important avant-garde groups of the sixties, surprisingly little comparative work has been published on the two movements. It appears that most 'experts' want to treat them as specialist areas which simply don't overlap. Although this book dealt with both groups, one of it's weaknesses was that it highlighted a few parallels between the two movements but failed to draw out the fact that through Gustav Metzger and the *Destruction In Art Symposium* (DIAS), we can find overlaps in the personnel who belonged to these dual avant-gardes.

Metzger was, of course, a participant in the *Festival of Misfits* and had a number of other connections with Fluxus artists – some of whom were involved in DIAS. His links with the SI are less direct but are to be found among the likes of former COBRA and Situationist theorist Constant, who ranked among the leadership of the Dutch Provos at the time they participated in DIAS. Another DIAS/SI connection is Enrico Baj. Although he was never a member of the Situationist International, Baj was part of the milieu from which it grew, having been a participant in Asger Jorn's International Movement For An Imaginist Bauhaus – the group whose merger with the Lettriste International (LI) constituted the formation of the SI. Baj also has connections with Mail Art, an outgrowth of Fluxus. There's a whole chapter dedicated to Mail Art in Baj's book *Impariano la Pittura* (Rizzoli, Milan 1985). Metzger actually invited the specto-Situationist International to participate in DIAS – but rather unsurprisingly, the Debordists refused to have anything to do with the event. Other connections between the Situationists and Fluxus could probably be traced through LI and SI member Alexander Trocchi. These would take two routes, Trocchi's beatnik connections dating back to the fifties and his involvement with the London underground of the sixties, when he was unsuccessfully attempting to launch *Project Sigma*.

Apart from failing to draw out these overlaps in personnel, the book is also weakened by the fact that I make no distinction between avant-garde and underground movements – the former tending to be much more ideologically coherent than the latter. As well as possessing a greater critical rigour, the avant-garde collects together in smaller and more exclusive groups than the loosely structured underground. The SI clearly constituted an avant-garde movement – as did the various tendencies which fed into it. Fluxus began its life as an avant-garde movement but degenerated into an underground current. The Dutch Provos, Motherfuckers, King Mob, Yippies, Mail Artists, Punks and Class War exhibit an underground rather than an avant-garde mentality. Neoism was self-consciously avant-garde. Although the Portland based founders of the group had intended to create an anti-ideological underground movement called No Ism, the young French Canadians who were among the first to take up the call issued by Dave Zack, Al Ackerman and Maris Kundzin, transformed the ideas of their mentors and in doing this, reinvented the avant-garde for the post-Punk generation. This process, which was one of almost complete reversal, resulted in the tendency being renamed Neoism. As perhaps the only genuinely avant-garde group of the ten year period between 1975 and 1985, the Neoists rank among the most likely candidates for future canonisation as part of the tradition that stretches from Futurism and Dada to the Situationists and Fluxus.

Possibly due to avant-garde personalities desiring what James H. Billington describes as 'radical simplification', the history of groups such as the Neoists and Situationists tends to become even more distorted than those of related underground movements. Obviously, this process has advanced a lot further in the case of the SI but it's also become an important factor in the historification of Neoism. A case in point is the chapter on the group in Geza Perneczky's *A Halo* (Hettorony Konyvkiado, Budapest 1991). In this text, Neoism is treated as if it had already arrived at its post-1984 stage of development when the Portland 3 founded the movement as No Ism in 1978. The book also devotes undue space to Istvan Kantor and me at the expense of an accurate history of the group. As a Hungarian émigré, Kantor was probably viewed as being of particular interest to those who spoke the language in which the book was published, while I provided the easiest means of linking Neoist theory back to that of the Situationist International. This is a mirror image of the way in which Situationism has been historified, since much of the published material on the SI continues to exhibit a bias against – or at least ignorance of – North and East European members of the group. In the

Anglo-American world, there has also been a complete misunderstanding of the way in which Situationist ideas were initially taken up by a handful of English speaking radicals.

According to legend, the men who 'invented' Punk Rock were former members of the English 'Situationist' group King Mob, who'd abandoned the revolutionary cause and instead perverted the ultimate anti-capitalist critique as a way of making money. The reality is rather different. The four members of what was briefly the English section of the Situationist International were part of a larger anarchist/freak scene in Notting Hill, West London. Their understanding of Situationism was filtered through pop culture, anarchism, black power, the underground and many other things – as can be seen from their extremely free translations of French Situationist texts. When the English section of the Situationist International was expelled by the mother lodge in Paris, they formed King Mob with Dave and Stuart Wise. Rather than being Situationist, King Mob was actually an imitation of the New York Motherfuckers group. A few of the individuals who were later active in the early Punk scene were on friendly terms with members of King Mob and other Notting Hill activists. This connection may have contributed to some of the wilder aspects of the sixties counterculture being incorporated into Punk – although none of the ideas that were passed from one generation to the next were explicitly Situationist. That this is also the official position of the Debordists is made quite clear by a very explicit comment in *Internationale Situationiste* 12: 'a rag called *King Mob*... passes, quite wrongly, for being slightly pro-situationist'.

The problems associated with the historification of the Situationist International were greatly compounded by the 1989 retrospective exhibition of their work. The show was tailored to please chauvinists in three different national markets – so that in Paris the exhibition more or less concluded with the French uprisings of May '68, in London with British Punk Rock and in Boston with American simulationist painting. While the protests of those who opposed the very idea of a Situationist retrospective seemed rather pointless – if the SI had not wished to be historicised by way of exhibitions, the group wouldn't have deposited documents with museums – it was a great pity that the show was completely deformed by nationalist considerations.

Much of what has been written about the SI simply consists of anecdotes from a mythologised history. Even the American journalist who tried to break out of this vicious circle by adopting a technique of free association, demonstrates little more than the failure of his own imagination by endlessly falling back on the key episodes of Strasbourg, May '68 &c. In *Lipstic Traces* (Secker & Warburg, London 1989), Greil Marcus moves effortlessly from John of Leyden (religious heresies of the middle ages) to Johnny Lydon (who under the pseudonym Rotten sang for the Sex Pistols) not simply due to the names sounding similar but because they make up what the author perceives as a hip and radical alternative history. The result is a sanitised Situationist family tree, the more unpleasant findings that ought to turn up given Marcus's technique of free association simply don't feature in the book. For example, the Council for the Liberation of Daily Life, who went on to become the American section of the SI, operated out of Box 666, Stuyvesant Station, New York – 666 is, of course, the number of the Beast or Satan. Likewise, Sid Vicious (bass player with the Sex Pistols) murdered his girlfriend in New York's Chelsea Hotel which many years earlier had hosted Ku Klux Klan meetings.

There are numerous parallels to be drawn between the SI and the far-Right. Many reactionaries not only write in a manner similar to the specto-Situationist house style, they're also drawn towards the same themes. Taken out of context, suitably censored chunks of ultra-rightist propaganda could be passed off as Debordist texts. Take, for example, a piece of writing by the notorious anti-Semite Douglas Reed: 'The money power and the revolutionary power have been set up and given sham but symbolic shapes ('capitalism' or 'communism') and sharply defined citadels ('America' or 'Russia'). Suitably to alarm the mass mind, the picture offered is that of blank and hopeless enmity and confrontation… Such is the spectacle publicly staged for the masses. But what if similar men with a common aim secretly rule in both camps and propose to achieve their ambitions through the clash between those masses? I believe that any diligent student of our times will discover that this is the case.' While, C. H. Douglas in the *Social Crediter* of 17th July 1948 sounds even more trenchantly Debordist : 'Ideas and even whole paragraphs… which first see the light in the *Social Crediter* can be read in increasing numbers in various reviews and periodicals… almost invariably without acknowledgement'.

The similarity between the rhetoric of assorted reactionaries and the SI is partially due to the Debordists finding themselves in the same political wilderness as economic cranks such as Major Douglas and his Social Credit movement. However, the parallels run far deeper than this and they can't be reduced to a single issue without grossly distorting our understanding of the subject. The SI plagiarised a number of slogans that had previously been popular among Christian heretics of the middle ages. The religious ideologies from which these epigrams sprang were virulently anti-Semitic and this gives us another angle from which we can look at the Situationist's relationship to the racist right. It's extraordinary that Marcus fails to mention this, since he cites a work – Norman Cohn's *The Pursuit of the Millenium* (rev. ed. Oxford, New York 1970) – which deals very explicitly with the anti-Semitic content of feudal heresies.

To return again to the technique of free association, although Marcus doesn't do much with it, the procedure can certainly produce interesting results. For instance, Charles Radcliffe, a member of the English section of the specto-Situationist International, shares his name with the Jacobite who is said to have founded the earliest Masonic Lodge in Paris and assumed the role of its first Grand Master in 1725. Thinking about the SI in terms of a Masonic organisation throws light on how the group functioned. There was no application procedure for individuals who wished to join the Situationist International, membership was a privilege offered only to those considered worthy of the honour. Asger Jorn appears anxious to dispel the idea that the SI is a latter day version of the Illuminati when he writes in *Situationiste Internationale* 5 (December 1960): 'The Situationists unilaterally reject the request made in Pauwels and Bergier's book *The Morning of the Magicians* (Les Matin des Magiciens), for assistance in setting up an institute to research occult techniques – and the formation of a secret society for those who are able to manipulate the conditions of their contemporaries'.

Despite Jorn's rejection of Bergier and Pauwels proposal, the Situationists were fascinated by the occult and this aspect of the movement has been largely overlooked by the individuals who've championed the SI in recent years. But as Graham Birtwistle notes in his book *Living Art* (Reflex, Utrecht 1986), while there 'is no evidence that Jorn associated himself with any theosophical movement in a way comparable to his membership of the Communist Party… his interest in esoteric traditions was certainly more than a passing fascination and in his later theories it was to wax while the orthodoxy of his Marxism was to wane'. When Jorn was asked in a 1963 interview if he was a shaman, he replied: 'Well, how is one to answer that… don't you know about the shamans?'.

James Webb devoted a few paragraphs to the Situationists and mysticism in his book *The Occult Establishment* (Open Court, Illinois 1976). Among other things, he noted that: 'The 'society of the spectacle' is seen as both cause and effect of the system of production, but it might quite simply be expressed as Maya, the illusion which must be overcome. Throughout all the transformations from Surrealism to Situationism, the idea of overcoming appearance has held constant: and traditional occultism and mysticism agree very well with this position. The new revolutionaries do not forget their masters. Andre Breton's last pronouncement on Surrealism cited the esotericist Rene Guenon – who began his career as a disciple of Papus – and the Situationist Raoul Vaneigem's *Traite de Savoir Vivre* (1967) actually includes a chapter with the same title as one of Guenon's books.'

From Ivan Chtcheglov's 1953 essay *Formulary for a New Urbanism* with it's references to Campanella ('there is no longer any Temple of the Sun') through to Debord's recent writing, the Situationist circle has been obsessed with the occult, mysticism and secret societies. The editors of the post-Situationist journal *Here and Now* hinted at this when they ran a parody of a Debord collage on the cover of their double issue 7/8 – prominently featured was a Rosicrucian bee-hive. Inside, there was a review of Debord's book *Commentaire sur la Societé du Spectacle* which was illustrated by a portrait of Adam Weishaupt, the eighteenth century founder of the Illuminati. The *Here and Now* editorial board appear to be suggesting that the SI emerge from three different traditions: one artistic, one political and a third which is largely ignored – that of the occult and secret societies. Since most 'secret' knowledge is non-verbal rather than actually being 'secret', it's appropriate that Mike Peters and his friends should allude to this largely unrecognised influence by the use of pictures.

At this point, it's perhaps illuminating to turn to a 1978 interview with Ettore

Sottsass Jr who was an integral part of the milieu that formed itself into the Situationist International: 'I was always interested in ancient cultures, the Egyptian, the Sumerian, the Central American and Jewish cultures… cultures that have left traces in our memories, from magic to religion to fanaticism. Technologies of life which are not always rational, like those of the East, which progress by constant training of the body and mind'. Of course, Sottsass broke with Jorn and Debord's circle just prior to the foundation of the SI and today this Italian is best known for the typewriters he designed while working at Olivetti and the furniture he's produced with 'Memphis'! However, his attitudes are typical of those who belonged to the SI, even after the movement split into rival 'cultural' and 'political' factions.

Like the Situationists, the Neoist Network drew heavily on the mythology of the occult and secret societies. Florian Cramer has been researching this area. In a letter to the author, Cramer stated that Kabbalism was a major influence on John Berndt's Neoist writings: 'Berndt quotes the concept of gematry, that is equating words with the numerical values of their letters… Other Neoists, such as tENTATIVELY a cONVENIENCE have produced work premised on this occult technique. You report in *The Assault on Culture* that tENTATIVELY substituted 'e' with '(nn)' in some of his texts: 'n' is the fourteenth letter in the alphabet, the total of the digits of fourteen is five, or 'e'. In *The Flaming Steam Iron*… Berndt writes that the perception of total incoherency leads to a new coherency (if 'no things are alike' then 'anything is anything') resulting in the materialisation of Monty Cantsin. This is the very problem the Kabbalah is concerned with. And Berndt continues: 'The Neoist universe of cosmology is based on the house of nine squares'. The square is the Kabbalist symbol of God and his four letter name is YHWE'.

The Scottish Neoist Pete Horobin once told me that Montreal activist Kiki Bonbon appropriated the word Neoism from a text by the notorious magus Aleister Crowley. The multiple identity Monty Cantsin, which was adopted by many members of the Neoist Network, was intended as an explicit reference to the Free Spirit movement of the middle ages. The name literally meant what it said – Monty Can't Sin! This was a standard heresy of the feudal era, which in less condensed form ran that because God was everywhere, everyone was God – and because God couldn't sin, there was no such thing as sin. Hell was simply refraining from doing the things that we desired – while blasphemy, drunkenness and fornication were holy acts.

More than anything else, Neoism was about transforming the way in which the everyday world was perceived, an attempt to subvert consensus reality. An anecdote about the *8th International Neoist Apartment Festival* in London will illustrate this far better than any amount of theory. On the final day of this event, two Hungarians knocked on the door of the Neoist HQ and asked if they could interview Istvan Kantor. Pete Horobin informed them that Kantor had returned to Montreal. After some further banter, the men were invited into the building and led through to the downstairs room where I was working on an audio document. The Hungarians were dressed in long raincoats and looked like caricatures of KGB agents. Their cover story was that they worked on a youth magazine in Budapest and had flown to London specifically to do a feature on Neoism. Since Horobin had single-handedly organised the Apartment Festival, he took it upon himself to explain what the event had been about, while I answered some questions about my involvement with the movement. Both Horobin and I refused to let the 'journalists' take our pictures. The Hungarians then requested permission to photograph the building. Upon being told that this was okay, they proceeded to take snaps of walls, doors and windows.

At this point, tENTATIVELY a cONVENIENCE came downstairs to find out what was going on. After being informed that the visitors were 'journalists', tENT offered to pose for a portrait. However, he didn't want the picture to be of his face, it had to feature the upside-down question mark that had been shaved into the back of his head. As one of the Hungarians aimed the camera, tENTATIVELY told him to wait a minute because he wanted the question mark to come out the right way up in the photo. tENT then attempted to stand on his head. After pretending that he was unable to do this, he got up and said he had another idea – if the camera was held upside down, the question mark would come out the right way up in the picture! The Hungarian obediently did as he was told.

Like the Lettristes, the Neoists were groping towards new modes of being – and the relationship between Neoism and the Plagiarist/Art Strike movement provides some remarkable parallels with Lettrisme's role as a precursor to the more significant Situationist International. This book didn't include chapters on the various *Festivals of Plagiarism* or the Art Strike because it would have been premature to write about them in 1987. I was very actively involved with the various Plagiarism/Art Strike groups and what I have to say about them can be found elsewhere. John Berndt, Florian Cramer, Geza Perneczky and several other individuals have been attempting to appropriate all the work I produced after breaking with Neoism for that earlier movement. They are particularly keen to claim late issues of my magazine *Smile* as Neoist publications. Possibly this is because they wish to present the Neoists as the last possible avant-garde. Berndt, for instance, produced posters proclaiming 'BEWARE: STEWART HOME IS STILL A NEOIST' and has suggested that within Neoism I played Henry Flynt to Dave Zack's George Maciunas.

Without doubt, former comrades are becoming increasingly bitter as the eighties avant-garde enters the history books in a suitably distorted fashion. An example of this process is to be found in the new standard English language work on anarchism, *Demanding the Impossible* by Peter Marshall (Harper Collins, London 1992): 'Inspired by the Situationists and anarchist theory another post-punk anti-authoritarian group emerged in the late 1980s around… journals like *Smile*, *Here and Now* and the more scholarly *Edinburgh Review*. Much of the new libertarian writing is in the Ranter and Dadaist tradition of poetic declamation. It fuses fact and fiction, history and myth, and opposes the primitive to the civilized. Rather than resorting to agit-prop, it tries to politicize culture and transform everyday life'.

Equally distorted accounts of the Neoist and Plagiarist movements can be found in the third edition of the *Glossary of Art, Architecture and Design Since 1945* by John A. Walker (London Library Association, 1992). Somewhat surprisingly, when the Victoria and Albert Museum organised an exhibition entitled *Smile: a Magazine of Multiple Origins* (London, March-August 1992) the accompanying catalogue essay by Simon Ford was remarkably accurate.

I now want to go back in time and deal with a few of the problems associated with the historification of Fluxus. Henry Flynt in his essay 'Mutations of the Vanguard: Pre-Fluxus, during Fluxus, late Fluxus' (included in *Ubi Fluxus, Ibi Motus 1990-1962*, catalogue to the Fluxus exhibition at the 1990 Venice Biennale) observes: 'In the process of transforming Fluxus into a reiterated museum exhibit, there has been an astonishing amount of manipulation of Fluxus history… All radical claims – aside from mere unpretentiousness – have been stripped from Fluxus. Also, a genuine Fluxus offshoot such as the Neoists has been blocked from official Fluxus because its members are undergrounders rather than money artists'.

Flynt goes on to suggest that Fluxus supremo George Maciunas was obsessed with the idea of organising the entire avant-garde – although obviously the greater part of it, such as the Situationist and Destruction In Art movements, escaped his control. However, as *Mutations of the Vanguard* makes clear, much of the New York scene which operated independently of Maciunas during the post-war period has now been assimilated into Fluxus through sleight of hand operations on the part of academics, curators and artists jostling for a place in the culture industry. Ironically, many of the Fluxus bandwagon jumpers were more successful than the Maciunas circle during the sixties – but now find themselves reduced to claiming membership of this 'historically important' movement because their own careers have flagged while what was formerly a marginal group has benefited from the 'vagaries' of fashion. The parallels between the historification of Fluxus and the Situationist International are remarkable. While in the late sixties and early seventies, it was Daniel Cohn-Bendit and the March 22nd Movement who were considered to be at the forefront of the May '68 uprisings in France, twenty-five years later, various enthusiasts have succeeded in transforming the image of the numerically insignificant Debordists from one of impotent ideologues whining on the sidelines to that of pivotal actors in the drama.

Returning to Flynt, I want to deal briefly with the claim he makes in his essay to the effect that after 1968 there was no longer any need for an avant-garde. Flynt's argument basically runs that once he had developed his critique of art and abandoned this area of activity in favour of 'brend' – paradoxically to resume work as an artist at the tail end of the eighties – the avant-garde was an anachronism. While brend was a more advanced concept than Debord's simplistic understanding of art as an essentially radical content that had been deformed by its bourgeois packaging, the necessarily subjective formulation of the Flyntian modality prevents it from acting as the last word on the avant-garde for anyone other than its author. In fact, the Art Strike movement of the late eighties took up elements of the critiques of culture made by Flynt, Metzger etc., and succeeded in propagating this heady brew with far greater success than any previous avant-garde group.

Staying close to the present, another movement not covered in the pages that follow was the Wroclaw based Orange Alternative. This was because news of what Waldemar Frydrych and his circle were doing did not reach my ears until after the first English edition of the book was published. Among the publicity generated by the Situationist exhibition in 1989, certain hacks saw fit to make passing reference to the Orange Alternative as Polish Situationists. From the scanty information available in English, this appeared to be mere hyperbole, since the few reports about the Wroclaw group that did appear in the Western press made it clear that the Orange Alternative had more in common with the underground traditions of the Dutch Provos and American Yippies, than with the SI's vanguard pretensions.

One action in particular, resonated with those who were familiar with the sixties counterculture in the West. It was reported that during a December demonstration, members of the Orange Alternative dressed up as Father Christmas – and that this caused a great deal of confusion among representatives of the Polish authorities. When the police attempted to round up the protesters, they also managed to arrest a number of those who'd been genuinely employed to play the role of Santa Claus. Two decades earlier, members of the New York Motherfuckers group had gone into a department store impersonating Santa Claus and handed out free gifts – with the result that the public were treated to the spectacle of the police snatching back toys from children and Father Christmas being arrested. Members of King Mob were so taken with the success of this scandal that they repeated it in London. However, while it's likely that at least some Orange Alternative activists were familiar with both Debordist theory and the sixties counterculture of the West, they clearly developed a praxis that reflected their unique social situation.

There are other groups around today that draw on the legacy of the avant-garde and underground movements described in this book. One example is the US based Immediast Underground. Personally, I'm not impressed by this outfit – their propaganda is little more than a contentless string of buzz words: 'Dealing with the Ecology of Coercion; Networker Congresses; Correspondence, Mail Art and Exchange; Hacking; Seizing the Media; Routing the Spectacle against itself; Creating Public Production Libraries; Enjoying Public Media and an Open State'. The Anti-Copyright Network (ACN) is an international group working in a similar area – they distribute subversive fly-posters around the globe. The claims the ACN makes for itself are more modest than those of the Immediast Underground but their activities are more substantial.

The London Psychogeographical Association (LPA) was initially no more than a name made up at the founding conference of the Situationist International to make the proceedings sound more impressive. In 1992, the group became a reality. I was alerted to this fact after being handed a leaflet that read: 'London Psychogeographical

Association trip to the Cave at Roisia's Cross, August 21st–23rd. This trip has been organised to coincide with the conjunction between Jupiter and Venus on 22 August. The trip will last for three days and involve cycling for about 100 miles and camping for two nights. The rendez-vous is at the back of Tesco's car park, Three Mills Lane, London E3 at 11am on Friday 21 August with bicycle and camping gear. We hope you can make it – see you there!'

A further outing was organised by the LPA to research the environs of St. Catherines Hill, Winchester, on the occasion of the conjunction of Venus, Uranus, Neptune and the Moon. A booklet entitled *The Great Conjunction: the Symbols of a College, the Death of a King and the Maze on the Hill* was published on the first day of this 36 hour excursion. The text revealed that the LPA was conducting rigorous investigations into ley-lines, the occult, the ritual organisation of power, alchemical psychodrama, mind control and architectural symbolism. The group is developing various avenues of research left unexplored by the Situationists after Asger Jorn left the movement and it split into two rival factions. The (re)formation of the LPA looks like being one of the most important events of recent years – it may revitalise the avant-garde.

Having looked at a few of the recent developments that grew from the tradition of oppositional culture described in the pages that follow, I want to get back to the task in hand and wrap up this introductory essay. Only a little more than five years have passed since I wrote this book but it seems like a lifetime. While the text has its faults, if I began to correct them there'd be no end to the process and I'd find myself writing a different work. In the words of one reviewer, the book is 'a concise introduction to a whole mess of troublemakers through the ages'. I like to think of the following pages as a bluff your way guide, a fairly painless means of getting an overview of the cultural currents in the second half of this century that owe a greater or lesser debt to the Futurists, Dadaists and Surrealists. The way the book is organised will become clear towards the end, everything hangs on two chapters – 'Beyond Mail Art' and 'Neoism'. If I was going to write a book devoted to just one of the movements that gets name checked in the chapter headings that follow, it would be Neoism. In particular, I'd like to research the claims made by various French-Canadian Neoists to the effect that they created the first computer viruses at the beginning of the eighties. Although the early date suggested for this accomplishment makes the claim appear rather dubious, it's probably only a matter of time before various enthusiasts start declaring that the entire hacker underground was a Neoist invention. However, there's absolutely nothing about this in the following pages, as you'll discover if you read on…

Stewart Home, London, January 1993

Selected Bibliography

INCLUSION IN THIS LIST does not mean the material is factually accurate. The pieces by Grant Kester and Geza Perneczky, in particular, are riddled with errors but remain of interest.

Ball, Edward: Just Say No, *Village Voice* 14/11/89.

Bennun, David: Suedehead Revisited, *Melody Maker* 9/10/93.

Cornwell, Jane: Carry On Class War, *i-D* November 1993.

Dodson, Mo: Meg And Sharon Get Laid, *New Statesman & Society* 8/12/89.

Feaver, William: Pink Feather Duster, Matching Fly-Swatter, *Observer* 14/12/86.

Ford, Simon: *Smile Classified*, catalogue accompanying exhibition at the Victoria & Albert Museum March/August 1992.

Henry, Clare: Art Tackles Aids Issue, *Glasgow Herald* 11/5/87.

Houghton, Nick: Ruining The Ruins, *Performance Magazine* 46 March/April 1987.

Kester, Grant: Smile Art Press Review, *New Art Examiner* October 1987.

Mabbott, Alastair: Art No More, *The List* 99, 26/7/89.

Orr, Deborah, Dada For Now, *Guardian* 29/1/93.

Perneczky, Geza: *The Magazine Network: the trends of alternative art in the light of their periodicals 1968-1988* (pages 161-173), Soft Geometry Koln 1993.

Phillpot, Clive: Artists' Magazines: news of the Art Strike, Monty Cantsin & Karen Eliot, *Art Documentation* Fall 1992.

Plant, Sadie: *The Most Radical Gesture: the Situationist International in a Postmodern Age* (pages 177-182), Routledge London & New York 1992.

Reynolds, Simon: Stewart Home Interview, *Melody Maker* 20/1/90.

Sale, Jonathan: All Whose Own Work? *Punch* 5/2/88.

Sinclair, Iain: Who Is Stewart Home? *London Review Of Books* 23/6/94.

Walker, John: Living In Borrowed Time, *Times Higher Education Supplement* 26/2/88.

Webb, Don: Neoism, *American Book Review* April/May 1994.

Wells, Steven: Home On The Deranged, *New Musical Express* 11/5/91.

Wells, Steven: Pity Politics, *New Musical Express* 16/10/93.

Williams, John: Artlaw, G-Spot 6 Spring 1993.

Index

STEWART HOME –

QUICK, CLEAN & EFFICIENT SINCE 1962

Red London

AK Press, A5 160pp £5.95

"It's a Richard Allen pulp hologram that Stewart Home is impersonating. But impersonation is too weak a term. It is more like a willed act of occult possession. William Blake becoming Milton so that he can recompose the older poet's faults."

Iain Sinclair, *London Review of Books*

No Pity

AK Press, A5 144pp £5.95

"Revolutionary polemic, violent, brutal, nauseating and bloody funny." *i-D*

"Speed-freak prose." *Melody Maker*

"Explicit beyond belief, fascinating in an ugly way, one step beyond most violent fiction." *The List*

Pure Mania

Polygon Books, A5 217pp £7.95

"A molotov cocktail of a novel. A switchback ride through an overamplified London lowlife of punch-ups, fast fucks and media hype. *Pure Mania* is the stuff of which cults are made." *Time Out*

Defiant Pose

Peter Owen, A5 167pp

£13.95 hardback

"Blunt, shocking and uncomfortable: a future underground classic." *The Face*

"The definitive cult novel." *NME*

The Assault on Culture – utopian currents from Lettrisme to Class War

AK Press, A5 128pp £5.95.

"A straightforward account of the vanguards that followed Surrealism: Lettrisme, Fluxus, Neoism and others even more obscure." *Village Voice*

Neoist Manifestos/ Art Strike Papers

AK Press, A5 112pp £5.95.

"Buy this book and you'll find out all you ever wanted to know about Neoism but were afraid to ask." *Edinburgh Review*

The Festival of Plagiarism

Sabotage Editions, A5 40pp

15 illustrations £1.95.

These books and many others are available from AK Distribution, 22 Lutton Place, Edinburgh EH8 9PE, Scotland, UK. Telephone 0131 667 1507. Please add 10% postage for UK orders (minimum 50p), 20% postage elsewhere (minimum £1). Cheques/postal orders/IMOs payable to AK Retail – these should be in sterling and drawn on a British bank or include a £6 fee to cover cashing charges. Payment may also be made in cash but this is at your own risk. AK US often has copies of these British publications available as imports, please write to AK Press, PO Box 40682, San Francisco, CA 94140-0682, USA or phone/fax 415 923 1429 for information about availability and prices..